HOW TO START AND
REALLY SUCCEED
in Your
OWN BUSINESS

A complete, easy-to-follow step-by-step guide covering everything
one needs to know to launch and succeed in their own business.
Habits that will make you Super Successful.

JON SPRANGER

This book is dedicated to my father, a visionary who lived decades ahead of his time. He instilled in me an unwavering belief that with dedication and focus, any goal is attainable. Thank you, Dad, for being my constant source of inspiration. You are, and always will be, the absolute best.

CONTENTS

INTRODUCTION

At 32, I leaped. I purchased a failing company that produced a unique air purification product substantially different from the mainstream options on the market. After deeply investigating, I saw a clear path to seizing a significant market share with the right design and marketing strategies. I was right. From hospital operating rooms to patient bedrooms and commercial spaces, the redesigned product line not only captured but also expanded the domestic and international markets. It's the only air cleaning/purifying product line to ever be registered by the U. S. Environmental Protection Agency. This was just the beginning.

Building from that success, at 37, I ventured into constructing and managing light industrial buildings, eventually amassing nearly one million square feet of rentable space. At 45, I sold my first building for a net profit of more than one million two hundred thousand dollars. Then, in 1999, I started a contract manufacturing firm for electronics, which mirrored the success of my previous ventures—flourishing into a highly profitable business.

Through these experiences, I've navigated the ups and downs of various industries, learning firsthand what it takes to succeed.

This book is crafted to guide, inspire, and equip you—the aspiring entrepreneur. Whether you're just contemplating your first venture or are knee-deep in your startup journey, this book is for you. It's tailored to help you lay a solid foundation, effectively launch your offerings, manage growth, and scale your operations to achieve lasting success.

You might be wondering, "Can I really do this?" Let me share a quick story from the early days of my first business. Shortly after taking over, I secured a new dealer whose initial order was substantial. However, I was shocked to discover our stock levels couldn't meet this order due to poor inventory management from the previous owner. I had to scramble, ordering parts overnight at exorbitant costs. This was a tough lesson right out of the gate, but it taught me the importance of proactive management and adaptability—qualities you will learn to develop throughout this book.

I'm here to show you that the path to business success while challenging, is attainable with the right approach. This book is packed with actionable frameworks, real-life applications, and interactive tools designed to tailor strategies to your unique business scenario.

Entrepreneurship is transformative. It's about envisioning success and making it happen through persistence, insight, and adaptability. As you turn these pages, I would like you to proceed with an open mind, ready to apply these lessons to your entrepreneurial journey.

The road to success begins with the step you're about to take. And let's turn your business dreams into reality.

NOW IS THE TIME TO TAKE ACTION TO SEE YOUR DREAM COME TRUE!! CONTINUE READING TO TAKE THAT FIRST STEP!

WE WILL START WITH A COMPLETE, EASY-TO-FOLLOW QUICK-START GUIDE

1. Begin by identifying a product or service that genuinely excites and impresses you. Visualize taking this product or service to market and building a successful company around it. You can achieve this by starting a new company, purchasing an existing one, partnering with an established business owner, or collaborating with someone who shares your entrepreneurial vision. (Chapters 1-2 & 3 will guide you through these initial steps towards building your successful company.)

2. To kickstart or acquire your business, financial resources are crucial. If you find yourself in need of additional support, consider reaching out to a successful business owner. Many of them are not just willing but eager to invest in and mentor individuals with the vision to start and build their own businesses. This mentorship can be a life-changing experience, as I discovered with my first company, where I met my mentor through the law firm I was working with to buy the business. (Chapter 4 will provide you with comprehensive details on various ways to fund your company.)

3. Your vision will guide you in taking your product or service to the market. One of the first strategic moves you can make is to establish your brand as the best in your marketplace. This can be achieved through meticulous consideration of your products, trademarks, brand names, and logos. Your distribution and advertising campaigns will play a pivotal role in this. (Chapters 5 & 6 will equip you with a complete overview of going to market.)

4. Depending on your business, you will need offices and even production facilities to build a product. I suggest you keep these as small and manageable as possible at the start. The same holds true for the number of employees you need to operate. The first company I bought was in 1,200 square feet with three employees, with sales of less than $50,000 a year. I grew that to 15,000 square feet with seven full-time employees, doing over 5 million dollars a year. (Chapter 7 will continue to guide you in these areas as your company grows.

5. You will need to decide on how to structure your company. The first company I bought was already a C Corporation, so I needed to learn everything about running a C Corporation. As you can see, we were highly successful with this structure, partly due to all of the global business we did. There is a lot of talk and information being put out on Limited Liability Companies or LLCs. While LLCs work for many situations, they do not work for all situations. I suggest you consult a law firm that specializes in business law and business taxation. Once you discuss your total business plans with them, they can advise you on the best way to structure your company and why you want to use that structure. (Chapter 8 will provide all of the relevant information based on current laws.)

6. YOU ARE NOW UP AND RUNNING. It's time to step back and examine where you are and where you want to go. It's time to lay out plans to grow and expand your company. Regular self-assessment and planning are key to business success. I suggest that this is always on your mind and part of your day-to-day thoughts in running your business. I recommend stopping at the end of every week and looking at where the week has taken your business. At the end of every 90 days, do an in-depth review of everything you think was good or bad. Enhance the good in every way you can and take whatever steps

are necessary to correct what you think was bad. At the end of every year, it is crucial that you step back and review the entire year in the same manner. After this review, you need to update your annual marketing plan incorporating all of the positive things you have learned and dealing with anything that did not work. (Chapters 9 & 10 will provide a wealth of information to help you in this area.)

YOU ARE NOW BECOMING THE BUSINESS PERSON YOU DREAMED OF – SUPER SUCCESS IS AT YOUR DOORSTEP!!

CHAPTER 1

CULTIVATING THE ENTREPRENEURIAL MINDSET CAPTURED AND EXPANDED

The leap from dreaming about a business to actually building one can often seem like a chasm too vast to cross. Yet, every successful entrepreneur has taken this exact leap. How, you might ask, does one transition from the comfort of thought to the reality of action? This initial chapter is dedicated to turning the key in the ignition of your entrepreneurial engine—from igniting the spark of your idea to setting it into full throttle.

In business, transforming from a dreamer to a doer isn't just about taking action. It's about cultivating a mindset that drives you forward, even when the path gets steep. Here, we delve into the psychological shift needed to set the stage for your business venture, equip you with strategies to overcome inertia, and teach you to visualize success vividly. These are steps and a new way to see and interact with your world. They will become the backbone of your entrepreneurial spirit.

1.1 FROM DREAMER TO DOER: ACTIVATING YOUR ENTREPRENEURIAL MIND

Identify Your Why: Understand the core motivations behind your desire to start a business.

Every monumental endeavor begins with a 'why.' Why do you want to start a business? Is it the freedom it offers, the potential financial rewards, or the chance to make a significant impact? I would like you to understand your fundamental motivations because they will serve as your anchor during challenging times. For instance, if your primary motivation is to innovate within the tech industry, this vision will keep you focused and resilient through the ups and downs of business cycles. Start by writing down your reasons. Reflect on them. This is not just an exercise; it's a blueprint of your inner drive.

Mindset Shift: Learn how to transition from a passive dreamer to an active doer.

Shifting your mindset begins with a decision to stop waiting for the 'right time' and start making the present moment the right time. A proactive mindset involves setting clear, actionable goals and breaking them into smaller, manageable tasks. Each task completed is a step closer to your dream. This shift also means embracing learning as a continual process—every setback is a lesson, not a failure. Engage with resources, connect with mentors, and immerse yourself in environments that challenge you to grow. This active approach transforms the landscape of entrepreneurship from daunting to doable.

Overcoming Inertia: Strategies to combat procrastination and take the first step.

Procrastination is often rooted in fear—fear of failure, fear of the unknown, or even fear of success. To combat this, start with setting tiny, almost trivial daily goals for your business. For example, if you aim to start an online store, your task for today might be researching successful online stores. Tomorrow, perhaps draft a rough business model. Small steps accumulate, and momentum builds. Utilize tools like scheduling and time-blocking to dedicate specific times for your business tasks, making them non-negotiable parts of your day.

Visualize Success: The importance of visualizing success to manifest your business goals.

Visualization isn't just about daydreaming of success; it's a practiced method of setting your subconscious in motion. Regularly visualize not just the end success but each step of the journey. Imagine engaging with your clients, negotiating deals, or innovating a new product. Sports psychologists have long used this technique to improve athletic performance, and it is equally powerful in entrepreneurship. This mental rehearsal primes your brain to act in ways that align with your visions of success, effectively programming your mind toward achieving your business goals.

As this chapter unfolds, remember that each concept discussed isn't just a suggestion but a critical component of the entrepreneurial fabric. They are designed to be revisited and refined as you move forward. Take these initial steps seriously, for they set the foundation for your business aspirations to be built and realized.

1.2 BUILDING RESILIENCE AGAINST FAILURE AND SETBACKS

Understanding Failure: Redefining failure as a stepping stone rather than an endpoint.

In the life of an entrepreneur, the perception of failure can either be a blockade or a gateway to more significant achievements. It all hinges on perspective. Early in my career, when a product line didn't perform as expected, rather than viewing it as a defeat, I saw it as a crucial learning opportunity. This shift in mindset is vital. Think of failure as a teacher, not as a tormentor. It's a natural part of the entrepreneurial process, providing invaluable insights that must be evident in success. For instance, when my first venture stumbled due to inadequate market research, it was a harsh but necessary revelation of the importance of understanding market needs. This experience was a stepping stone that led to enhanced strategies in future projects, contributing significantly to the refinement of my business acumen. Embrace failure as a stepping stone by systematically reviewing what went wrong, understanding why it did, and figuring out how to adjust your strategies moving forward. This approach mitigates the sting of failure, fortifies your resolve, and refines your business methods.

Resilience Techniques: Practical techniques to build resilience and bounce back from setbacks.

Resilience in entrepreneurship is more than enduring; it's about adapting and thriving. One effective technique is to maintain a resilience journal. In this journal, record daily reflections on what went well, what didn't, and how you responded to different challenges. Over time, this journal will highlight patterns in challenges and your responses and show your growth in handling difficult situations. Another technique is to set incremental goals that lead to larger objectives. This method helps maintain momentum, even in tough times, by celebrating small victories and contributing to big successes. During the launch of my second company, when construction delays seemed to stall progress, focusing on completing smaller project milestones kept the team motivated and the project moving forward. Additionally, practice mental and physical wellness. Entrepreneurship is as much a mental game as it is a strategic one. Regular exercise, adequate rest, and mindfulness practices like meditation can significantly bolster psychological resilience, helping you maintain clarity and calm in business upheavals.

Learning from Mistakes: How to analyze and learn from failures to improve future strategies.

Learning from mistakes is a fundamental skill for any successful entrepreneur. Start by fostering an environment—whether it's just you or your team—where mistakes are openly discussed and not feared. When a mistake occurs, conduct a 'post-mortem' analysis. This involves examining the decision-making process, actions, and outcomes. Identify at what point things went awry and why. For example, if a marketing campaign fails to attract the anticipated audience, analyze the campaign's reach, message clarity, and audience engagement. Was the research on the target audience comprehensive? Was the message conveyed clearly? Understanding these facets can sharpen your marketing strategies moving forward. Additionally, involve your team in this learning process to enhance collective insight and problem-solving skills. This improves business strategies and encourages a culture of continuous improvement.

Creating a Support Network: The role of mentors, peers, and supportive communities in resilience.

No entrepreneur is an island; building a robust support network is crucial for sustained resilience. With their experience and wisdom, mentors can offer guidance, serve as sounding boards, and provide emotional support during challenging times. Peers, conversely, can relate to your entrepreneurial struggles and offer insights from their own experiences. Moreover, engaging with entrepreneurial communities can expand your resources, provide networking opportunities, and expose you to different perspectives and strategies. To build this network, start by contacting local business groups, attending industry conferences, and participating in online forums related to your business field. For instance, in my early days, joining a local entrepreneurs' group provided support and critical business connections that were instrumental in the scaling phase of my business. Remember, the strength of your network can be a significant factor in the resilience of your entrepreneurial career, offering both professional guidance and personal support.

1.3 TIME MANAGEMENT MASTERY FOR ASPIRING ENTREPRENEURS

Effective time management is the scaffolding that supports all entrepreneurial endeavors. It's about making the most of your hours without letting your business consume every waking moment—a crucial yet challenging balance. Let's explore concrete strategies that have helped me manage my time and ensured that my businesses thrived without sacrificing my personal life.

Prioritization Techniques: How to prioritize tasks effectively for maximum productivity.

In the dynamic world of entrepreneurship, the ability to prioritize tasks is not just helpful—it's essential for survival and success. The key lies in distinguishing between what is urgent and crucial, a concept popularized by President Dwight D. Eisenhower, which led to the development of the Eisenhower Box used in time management. Every task is evaluated and placed into categories: urgent and important, important but not urgent, urgent but not necessary, and neither urgent nor essential. This method has guided me through countless decisions, helping me focus on tasks that genuinely move the needle—like strategic planning and networking—while delegating or delaying less critical tasks. Moreover, I start each day by identifying the top three functions with the most significant impact. This focus ensures that the most crucial tasks receive my attention and energy, even when not everything goes to plan. This method isn't just about getting through your to-do list; it's about ensuring it matters to your business's growth and personal development.

Eliminating Time Wasters: Identifying and eliminating activities that drain time and energy.

One of the most enlightening exercises I've done as an entrepreneur is conducting a time audit on myself. For one week, I tracked how I spent every hour of my day, from the first-morning coffee to turning off the lights at night. The insights were eye-opening. I found that substantial chunks of time were being eaten up by tasks that could be automated or delegated or needed a clear plan for the day. Email, for instance, is a notorious time sink. To combat this, I set specific times for checking email—once midmorning and once in the late afternoon—so that constant alerts don't disrupt my day. Social media is another area where time can easily slip away. I tackled this by using apps limiting my time spent on social media during work hours, ensuring that my time online was intentional and productive. Identifying these time wasters and setting boundaries has been crucial in reclaiming hours better spent on high-impact business activities or enjoying well-deserved downtime.

Tools and Apps: Leveraging technology to manage your time more efficiently.

In today's digital age, technology offers tools to streamline time management for busy entrepreneurs. From project management software like Asana and Trello to communication tools like Slack, these resources have been indispensable in keeping my teams and projects on track without constant meetings or check-ins. I leverage tools like Calendly for scheduling to avoid the back-and-forth often associated with setting up meetings. I use Pomodoro timers for focus and productivity—simple yet effective in keeping me focused on tasks for short bursts, with scheduled breaks to avoid burnout. Furthermore, cloud-based document and data management systems such as Google Drive allow me to access my work from anywhere, at any time, which maximizes my productivity and ensures that I can make the most of my time, whether I'm in the office, on a plane, or working from home.

Balancing Work and Life: Strategies for maintaining a healthy work-life balance as an entrepreneur.

Maintaining a healthy balance between work and personal life is one of the most challenging aspects of entrepreneurship. Early in my career, I learned the hard way that all work and no play isn't sustainable. It wasn't just my personal life that suffered; my work did, too. To manage this, I've made it a priority to schedule time for non-work activities that replenish my energy—be it a morning run, reading, or spending time with family and friends. I treat these activities with the same importance as business meetings—they are immovable appointments on my calendar. This practice has not only improved my well-being but has also enhanced my productivity and creativity. Another strategy that has worked well for me is setting clear boundaries with my team about availability. Outside of emergencies, I discourage after-hours communication, which respects my time and that of my team, fostering a culture where personal time is valued and respected. These boundaries ensure that I am fully present and effective when working, and the same goes for my time off.

1.4 DEVELOPING A VISION THAT DRIVES SUCCESS

Crafting a clear, compelling vision for your business is akin to setting coordinates in a navigation system before a journey. Without this, you might find yourself wandering or, worse, moving in circles. A well-defined vision acts as a north star, guiding your business decisions and aligning your team's efforts toward a common goal. In the early days of my first company, the vision was simple yet ambitious: to revolutionize the air purification market with innovative, high-quality products. This vision was a statement and a clarion call that rallied our team, informed our product development, and shaped our marketing strategies.

Creating such a vision starts with understanding the broader impact you want your business to have. Ask yourself: What change do I want to bring to the industry? How do I envision the future of this business? What legacy do I want to leave? The answers to these questions will help you frame an aspirational and actionable vision. For instance, if you aim to launch a sustainable clothing brand, your vision could be to lead the fashion industry towards zero waste. This clear vision will inspire you and attract customers, partners, and investors who share your values.

Setting SMART Goals: How to set Specific, Measurable, Achievable, Relevant, and Time-bound goals.

To translate your vision into reality, it is crucial to set SMART goals. This acronym stands for Specific, Measurable, Achievable, Relevant, and Time-bound, each a critical pillar that turns vague ambitions into clear targets. Let's break it down using the example of expanding a business:

- **Specific**: Your goal should be clear and precise. Instead of saying, "I want to grow my business," specify, "I want to increase my customer base."

- **Measurable**: Attach a number to it. "I want to increase my customer base by 30%."

- **Achievable**: Given your resources and constraints, Please ensure the goal is realistic. If your business has grown at 5% annually, a 30% jump might only be achievable with significant changes or investments.

- **Relevant**: I want you to know that the goal must align with your broader business vision and objectives.

- Increasing your customer base should contribute to your overall vision of market leadership.

- **Time-bound**: Set a deadline. "I aim to increase my customer base by 30% within the next year."

Setting SMART goals creates a framework for focused action and practical steps toward achieving your business vision. Each goal acts like a stepping stone, building upon the previous one and propelling your business forward systematically and strategically.

Aligning Actions with Vision: Ensuring daily actions and decisions align with your overarching vision.

Aligning daily actions with your vision is what separates dreamers from successful entrepreneurs. This alignment ensures that every task, no matter how small, contributes to the bigger picture. In practice, this might mean turning down lucrative opportunities that don't fit your vision. For instance, if your vision involves promoting eco-friendly products, partnering with a company with questionable environmental practices could be more detrimental than beneficial, regardless of the immediate financial gain.

You can regularly review your business activities and decision-making processes to maintain this alignment. Ask yourself whether these actions help or hinder your progress toward your vision. This constant evaluation might seem tedious, but it instills discipline and ensures your business remains on the right track. Additionally, use your vision as a criterion for decision-making. Before making a decision, evaluate its impact on your vision. This approach simplifies decisions and ensures your business evolves in the right direction.

Communicating Your Vision: Techniques for effectively communicating your vision to stakeholders.

Communicating your vision effectively is crucial for internal alignment and external engagement. Your team needs to understand and believe in the vision and work towards it passionately. Meanwhile, investors, partners, and customers are more likely to support your business if they connect with your vision. To communicate effectively, you should start by articulating your vision clearly and compellingly. Use simple language and powerful imagery that conveys both the purpose and passion behind your vision. For instance, instead of saying, "We sell durable and affordable furniture," say, "We are creating cozy homes for everyone with furniture that lasts for generations."

Furthermore, integrate your vision into all aspects of your business communications—from your website and social media to your advertising and PR. Make your vision a part of your brand story consistently across all platforms. Additionally, reinforce your vision in your internal communications. Regularly discuss how your team's efforts contribute to the vision, celebrate milestones that bring you closer, and always link back to the vision in team meetings, newsletters, and company updates. This constant reinforcement keeps the vision alive and embeds it into the fabric of your corporate culture, making your business a living embodiment of your vision.

Your vision is your anchor and compass in navigating the often turbulent waters of entrepreneurship. It grounds you, guides, and galvanizes your team to push boundaries and achieve greatness. Please keep your vision in mind as you continue this book, for it is the beacon that will help you succeed.

1.5 THE ART OF DECISION-MAKING UNDER UNCERTAINTY

In business, uncertainty is as much a part of the landscape as innovation and competition. The ability to make sound decisions amid this uncertainty often separates thriving enterprises from those that falter. The key is not just to tolerate uncertainty but to embrace it—seeing it as a spectrum of possibility rather than a barrier to action. Through my experiences, from launching new products to navigating market shifts, I've learned that the crux of decision-making under uncertainty is not about achieving perfect clarity but rather about managing risks intelligently and making the best decisions with the information.

Embracing Uncertainty: Learning to be comfortable making decisions in uncertain environments.

Embracing uncertainty begins with acknowledging that not every variable can be controlled or predicted. This acceptance doesn't equate to resignation but empowers you to focus on what you can influence. Early in my career, when I decided to expand to a new market, the lack of precise data on market reception could have been a roadblock. Instead, I chose to view it as a challenge to innovate our approach. We started small, tested the waters with pilot projects, and gathered as much feedback as possible. This iterative approach allowed us to gradually dispel uncertainty and build a robust strategy based on real-world insights. Embracing uncertainty in this way turns it from a paralyzing factor to a stepping stone, using each decision as an opportunity to learn and refine your strategies.

Risk Assessment: How to assess risks and make informed decisions.

Practical risk assessment is pivotal in navigating uncertainty. It begins with identifying potential risks—financial, operational, market-related, or otherwise—and evaluating their likelihood and potential impact. This evaluation should not be a one-time activity but a continuous process, adapting as conditions change. For instance, when considering a new supplier, beyond the initial quality and cost assessments, I consider factors like supplier stability, geopolitical factors, and even environmental policies that could impact supply chains down the line. Tools like SWOT analysis (assessing strengths, weaknesses, opportunities, and threats) and risk matrices can be invaluable here, helping to visualize and prioritize risks, ensuring that you are not just reacting to risks as they come but actively preparing for them.

Intuition vs. Analysis: Balancing gut instinct with analytical thinking in decision-making.

Balancing intuition and analysis is like blending art and science. Your instincts, honed by experiences and insights, can often lead you to swift decisions when time is of the essence. On the other hand, analytical thinking, grounded in data and systematic evaluation, provides a solid foundation for your choices. The key is understanding when to rely more heavily on one over the other. For example, choosing a brand logo might heavily leverage an intuitive understanding of what resonates with your audience, while deciding on a business location should be more heavily weighted towards analytical factors like foot traffic data, demographic analysis, and cost calculations. When both factors are crucial, I often use a phased approach: initial instincts guide the exploratory phase, and rigorous analysis informs the final decision. This balance ensures that decisions are fast and efficient but also robust and defensible.

Scenario Planning: Preparing for multiple outcomes to minimize the impact of wrong decisions.

Scenario planning is essential in the decision-making arsenal, particularly under uncertainty. It involves envisioning various future scenarios—best case, worst case, and several in between—and planning responses accordingly. This method not only prepares you for different eventualities but also helps highlight the different risks and opportunities each scenario presents. For instance, when entering a new market, I develop scenarios varying from rapid adoption to lukewarm reception and plan different marketing and operational strategies for each. This preparation ensures that no matter how the market reacts, we are not caught off guard but can respond swiftly and effectively. Moreover, scenario planning helps build resilience, as it trains your organization to be adaptable and responsive, qualities invaluable in the fast-paced business world.

Navigating the murky waters of uncertainty in business requires courage, creativity, and meticulous planning. By embracing uncertainty, assessing risks intelligently, balancing intuition with analysis, and preparing for multiple scenarios, you equip yourself to survive and thrive in the face of ambiguity. These strategies do not remove uncertainty but provide you with a toolkit to manage it proactively, turning potential threats into opportunities for growth and learning. As you apply these principles, decision-making becomes less about avoiding wrong turns and more about charting a confident course through the unknown, ready to adapt and capitalize on whatever lies ahead.

CHAPTER 2

VALIDATING YOUR BUSINESS IDEA

Imagine standing at a crossroads with numerous paths unfurling before you. Each path represents a potential business idea, and choosing the right one can feel both exhilarating and daunting. This chapter is dedicated to validating your business idea, like selecting the most promising path and ensuring it leads you toward success and fulfillment. Validation is not just about affirming that your idea is good; it's about proving that it's viable, desirable, and capable of thriving in a competitive marketplace. Let's dive into crafting a value proposition that resonates deeply with your target audience, setting the stage for a business that's not only profitable but also impactful.

2.1 CRAFTING A VALUE PROPOSITION THAT RESONATES

Defining Your Value Proposition: Clarifying what differentiates your business from the competition.

Your value proposition is the cornerstone of your business identity. It's a clear statement that explains how your product or service solves problems or improves situations, delivers specific benefits, and tells the ideal customer why they should buy from you and not from the competition. To define a compelling value proposition, list your product's key benefits. For instance, if you are launching a new eco-friendly cleaning product, some benefits might include non-toxic ingredients, effectiveness in removing stains, and safety around pets and children. Next, identify what makes these benefits valuable from the customer's point of view. Perhaps your target customers are environmentally conscious parents who need safe, effective cleaning solutions. The connection between their needs and your product's benefits lies at the heart of your value proposition. It's about intersecting what you offer with what your customers crave.

Target Customer Needs: Identifying and understanding the needs of your target customers.

Understanding your customer's needs is critical to creating a product that truly resonates with them. This understanding begins with customer segmentation—dividing your potential customers into groups based on age, location, behavior, and lifestyle choices. For each segment, develop personas that represent your ideal customers. These personas should include demographic data, interests, and behavioral traits. For instance, one of your personas might be a middle-aged, health-conscious individual who prefers eco-friendly products and shops online. To gather this information, utilize surveys, interviews, and social media analytics.

Engaging with potential customers can provide invaluable insights into their needs, preferences, and pain points. This deep understanding enables you to tailor your value proposition directly to the desires and needs of your target audience, making your product indispensable to them.

Articulating Benefits: How to communicate your product or service's benefits.

Articulating the benefits of your product or service must go beyond simply listing features. It's about framing these features in a way that connects emotionally and logically with your potential customers. Start by identifying each feature of your product or service. Next, ask yourself, "What does this feature do for my customer?" This question helps transform a feature into a benefit. For instance, if one of the features of your eco-friendly cleaning product is that it's made from 100% natural ingredients, the benefit is safety and peace of mind for users concerning their family's health and wellbeing. To articulate these benefits effectively, use clear, concise language that resonates with your audience's values and communicates the real-world impact of your product. Customers don't buy features; they buy solutions to their problems. They buy feelings. They buy outcomes.

Testing Your Value Proposition: Methods to test and refine your value proposition with real customers.

Testing your value proposition ensures it aligns with customer expectations and market demands before a full-scale launch. Start with qualitative testing by sharing your value proposition with a small group of target customers. Get feedback through focus groups, in-depth interviews, or even informal conversations. Listen carefully to how customers perceive your value proposition and watch for signs of confusion or disinterest, indicating that further refinement is needed. Next, employ quantitative methods by creating simple online ads or email campaigns that test different versions of your value proposition. Measure engagement, click-through, and conversion rates to see which version resonates best with your audience. This data-driven approach not only refines your value proposition but also enhances your overall marketing strategy, ensuring that when you do launch, your product meets the market with precision and appeal.

By meticulously defining, understanding, articulating, and testing your value proposition, you set the foundation for a business that not only enters the market with confidence but also continues to thrive amidst competition and changing consumer preferences. Remember, your value proposition is more than a statement—it's a promise to your customers. A promise that your business lives up to every day, with every transaction and every customer interaction. Keep refining this promise as you progress, making it more robust, precise, and compelling. This is how you build a brand that people trust and champion.

2.2 THE LEAN STARTUP APPROACH: BUILDING AN MVP

The Lean Startup methodology, pioneered by Eric Ries, revolutionized how entrepreneurs think about launching businesses. Its core premise is to minimize the risk of business failure by maximizing learning through rapid, iterative product releases. This approach challenges the traditional model of spending years perfecting a product without honest customer feedback. Instead, it emphasizes the development of a Minimum Viable Product (MVP)—a basic version of your product that includes only the features necessary to satisfy early adopters and validate your business concept.

Developing an MVP is your first real test as an entrepreneur under the Lean Startup model. Start by identifying the core problem your product addresses. What do you think is the easiest way to solve this problem? This solution becomes your MVP. For example, suppose you are developing an app to help people track personal fitness goals. In that case, your MVP might include just enough features for users to log workouts and monitor progress, omitting more complex functionalities like social sharing or detailed analytics for now. The goal is not to launch a perfect product but to bring a functional solution to market as quickly as possible to begin the learning process.

Once your MVP is live, the real work begins. This stage involves setting up efficient feedback loops to gather insights from your users' experiences. This involves more than just collecting data; it requires a system to quickly analyze and act on this information. Implement tools to track user interactions, gather feedback through surveys or direct interactions, and monitor how the product is used. Each piece of feedback is a goldmine of information, providing a clear direction on what works, what doesn't, and what could be improved. For instance, if users of your fitness app frequently abandon their workout logs before completion, this might indicate that the data entry process is too cumbersome or the user interface is not intuitive.

The ability to pivot or persevere is the most critical decision you will make based on the feedback on your MVP. A pivot involves fundamentally changing your product based on feedback that your original hypothesis is not viable. This could mean changing the feature set, altering the user interface, or even overhauling the product's target audience. Persevering, on the other hand, means staying the course, perhaps making only minor adjustments. For example, suppose feedback reveals that users find the app's workout logging feature valuable but are frustrated by its complexity. In that case, a pivot might involve simplifying the feature rather than enhancing it. Alternatively, suppose the feedback is generally positive, and users engage with the app as expected. In that case, you may persevere and continue enhancing the product according to the original plan.

Navigating this decision-making process requires a balanced approach, blending data-driven insights with strategic foresight. The key is to avoid getting too attached to your initial ideas but to remain focused on solving your customers' problems effectively and efficiently. This adaptive route mitigates risks and increases the likelihood that your business will successfully meet market demands and achieve sustainable growth. As you iterate through cycles of feedback and refinement, remember that each loop brings you closer to a product that truly resonates with your target market, paving the way for a business loved by its customers and viable in the long-term market landscape.

2.3 MARKET RESEARCH TECHNIQUES FOR THE BOOTSTRAPPED ENTREPRENEUR

When embarking on your entrepreneurial path, understanding the landscape in which your business will operate is crucial. This understanding is primarily gained through effective market research, which, contrary to popular belief, does not have to drain your resources. For entrepreneurs with limited budgets, there are numerous ways to conduct thorough market research without breaking the bank. One approach is to utilize online surveys and polls through platforms like SurveyMonkey or Google Forms, which can be distributed across your social media channels or directly to your email list. This method not only helps gather quantitative data about potential customer preferences, behaviors, and demographics but also engages your audience and makes them feel involved in the development of your business. Another cost-effective strategy is analyzing data from government databases, industry reports, and case studies, which often contain valuable insights about market trends, consumer behavior, and competitive landscapes. These resources can provide a solid foundation for your market understanding without expensive primary research.

As you gather this data, your next step is to analyze market trends that could influence your business. This analysis involves looking beyond the surface data and understanding the underlying factors driving market shifts. Tools like Google Trends or industry-specific publications can provide insights into what is trending in your sector. For instance, if you are starting an organic snack company, you might find an increasing trend in organic food consumption and a growing consumer preference for gluten-free products. By identifying these trends early, you can position your business to meet emerging demands. Additionally, trend analysis can help you anticipate future changes in the market, allowing you to adapt your business model proactively rather than reactively. This forward-thinking approach prepares you to meet your market's evolving needs and positions you as a leader in innovation within your niche.

Another pivotal aspect of market research is conducting customer interviews. These interviews provide qualitative insights that surveys and data analysis cannot capture. Start by identifying a diverse group of potential customers, including those who directly fit your target demographic and peripherally related ones. Prepare open-ended questions encouraging detailed responses, such as "What challenges do you face when using current products in the market?" or "What would make our product more appealing to you?" Conversationally conduct these interviews, allowing for natural digressions that may uncover additional insights. This direct interaction gives you a deeper understanding of customer needs and preferences and builds relationships with potential early adopters of your product. The insights gained from these conversations can be compelling, often leading to pivotal shifts in product design or marketing strategies that more closely align with customer desires.

Lastly, competitive analysis is essential to understand your standing relative to others in the market. This process involves identifying your main competitors and evaluating their strengths and weaknesses. Begin by compiling a list of competitors, including direct competitors who offer similar products and indirect competitors who satisfy the same customer needs with different products. Visit their websites, analyze their marketing strategies, and use their products. Tools like SEMrush or Alexa can provide data on website traffic, keyword rankings, and online market share, indicators of a competitor's online strength. Additionally, customer reviews on platforms like Amazon, Yelp, or Google can provide unfiltered insights into what customers appreciate or dislike about your competitors' offerings. This analysis helps you find gaps in your competitors' strategies that your business can capitalize on. For instance, if competitor reviews consistently point out poor customer service, this is an area where your business could excel and differentiate itself. By thoroughly understanding your competition, you anticipate their moves and position your company to uniquely meet customer needs and preferences, carving out your niche in the marketplace.

Integrating these low-cost, high-impact market research techniques into your business planning lets you understand where your business stands and needs to go. This process is not just about collecting data; it's about turning insights into actionable strategies that drive your business forward, ensuring that your venture enters the market with a strong foundation and continues to thrive amid changing conditions and competition.

2.4 UTILIZING FEEDBACK LOOPS TO REFINE YOUR BUSINESS IDEA

Establishing Feedback Mechanisms: Setting up systems to collect continuous customer feedback.

In the dynamic business landscape, staying attuned to customer feedback is not just beneficial—it's essential for survival and growth. Establishing robust feedback mechanisms allows you to capture the voice of the customer continuously, providing insights that can drive strategic decisions and foster product enhancements. One effective way to collect ongoing feedback is through digital platforms that interact with your customers regularly. This could be as simple as an automated email that follows a purchase, asking for customer feedback, or more complex systems like in-app feedback tools that prompt users to rate features or report issues in real-time.

Additionally, leveraging social media as a two-way communication channel can provide a steady stream of feedback and foster a more personal connection with your audience. Platforms like Twitter, Facebook, and Instagram allow customers to leave comments, share experiences, and suggest improvements. To systematically capture this data, consider using social media monitoring tools to track mentions, tags, and keywords related to your brand. These tools help collect data and analyze sentiment, which can be particularly useful in gauging overall customer satisfaction and brand perception.

Setting up these systems requires an initial investment in the right tools and processes, but the payoff is substantial. Integrating feedback mechanisms into every customer interaction ensures that your business remains responsive and adaptive to customer needs, which is crucial in today's fast-paced market environments. Moreover, this ongoing dialogue with your customers builds trust and loyalty, as customers feel valued and heard, knowing that their input directly influences the products or services they use.

Analyzing Feedback: How to analyze feedback and extract actionable insights.

Collecting feedback is only the first step; the real magic lies in how you analyze this information to extract actionable insights. Data collected from various feedback channels can be voluminous and varied, making it seem daunting initially. However, by employing structured analytical methods, you can sift through this data effectively to uncover trends, patterns, and specific areas needing attention. Start by categorizing feedback into product usability, customer service, pricing, etc. This segmentation helps identify which areas are performing well and which are not, allowing you to allocate resources more effectively.

Consider using text analytics software to analyze open-ended responses for a more granular analysis. These tools can help identify common keywords and phrases, perform sentiment analysis, and even detect emotions, providing deeper insights into customer attitudes and feelings toward your product or service. For instance, if many users mention that a product is "hard to use," this could indicate a usability issue requiring redesign or additional user training.

Additionally, prioritize feedback based on its potential impact on your business. For example, issues affecting a large segment of your customer base or potential legal and safety concerns should be handled as soon as possible. Less critical feedback that involves minor enhancements or aesthetic changes can be scheduled for future updates. This prioritization ensures that your response to feedback is strategic and efficient, maximizing the positive impact on your business.

Iterative Improvement: Applying feedback to improve your product or service.

The heart of a feedback loop is its cyclical nature, where feedback is gathered, analyzed, and acted upon, leading to continuous improvements. This iterative process is guided by agile development principles, where enhancements are made in small, manageable increments rather than through extensive, infrequent updates. This approach allows for quicker responses to feedback and reduces the risk associated with significant changes.

When applying feedback to your product or service, start by mapping out the most critical changes that need to be addressed based on the analysis. Develop a clear action plan detailing what changes will be made, who will be responsible, and the timeline for implementation. It's also important to communicate these changes to your customers, particularly those who provided the feedback. This closes the loop and reinforces the value of their input, enhancing customer satisfaction and loyalty.

As these changes are implemented, please continue to monitor their impact. Set up key performance indicators (KPIs) related to changes, such as improved user satisfaction scores, increased usage, or reduced complaints. Monitoring these KPIs will help you understand whether the changes are having the desired effect and provide insights into further refinements that may be necessary. This ongoing feedback, analysis, and improvement process becomes a powerful engine for innovation and adaptation, keeping your product or service at the forefront of market needs and expectations.

Building a Community: Engaging early adopters to create a community around your product.

Early adopters are your initial customers and most valuable allies in refining and promoting your business. These users see your product's potential early on and are often keen to contribute to its development. Engaging these users by building a community around your product can be tremendously beneficial. Start by creating exclusive online or in-person forums where early adopters can interact with each other and your team. These forums can serve as a rich source of in-depth feedback and help foster a sense of belonging among users, which is crucial for building brand loyalty.

Offer incentives for participation in these communities, such as access to beta versions of the product, discounts on future purchases, or the opportunity to influence product development decisions. These incentives encourage engagement and make the community members feel valued and respected as contributors to your product's journey.

Furthermore, openly celebrate your community's successes and milestones. Whether it's a user who provided critical feedback that led to a significant product improvement or someone who frequently helps other users in the community, acknowledging these contributions can motivate ongoing engagement and support. This celebration helps transform your early adopters into brand ambassadors who continue to provide valuable insights and promote your product through word-of-mouth, which can be incredibly effective in attracting new customers.

Building a community around your product creates a feedback-rich environment that fosters continuous improvement and deepens customer relationships. This community becomes vital to your product's ecosystem, contributing to its refinement, growth, vibrancy, and appeal in the marketplace.

2.5 UNDERSTANDING YOUR COMPETITIVE EDGE

In the bustling marketplace where new businesses sprout daily, the question is more than whether you can enter the market or sustain and grow within it. This sustainability often hinges on your ability to carve out a unique competitive edge. This edge is not just about being different; it's about being irreplaceable in the eyes of your customers. Let's go ahead and explore how to crystallize this edge and make it a cornerstone of your business strategy.

Identifying Your USP: Identifying your Unique Selling Proposition that sets you apart.

Your Unique Selling Proposition (USP) is the one thing that makes your business better than the competition. A specific benefit makes your business stand out in a crowded market. Identifying your USP starts with deep introspection and a bit of market savvy. What do you offer that no one else can? It could be an innovative product feature, an unprecedented service model, or an exceptional customer experience. For example, suppose you are launching a new coffee shop in a crowded urban area. In that case, your USP might be the exclusive use of organic, locally sourced coffee beans combined with a pay-it-forward system that appeals to the community-minded urbanite. This USP sets you apart and embeds your business into the local community fabric, making your coffee shop a preferred destination.

To identify this selling point, you often need to look beyond the obvious and consider your customers' deeper needs and desires. This might involve enhanced customer research, competitive analysis, and even trial and error with your product offerings. Once identified, your USP should become the focal point of all your marketing messages and business decisions, consistently communicated across all platforms, from your website to your storefront. It's what you want your business to be known for, the promise that draws customers in and keeps them coming back.

Leveraging Competitive Gaps: Find and leverage gaps in the market your competitors still need to include.

While identifying your USP is about highlighting your strengths, leveraging competitive gaps involves turning your competitors' weaknesses into opportunities. This strategy requires you to be both observant and opportunistic. Start by thoroughly analyzing your competitors' offerings, customer reviews, and market performance. Look for patterns or recurring complaints that indicate a gap in their offerings. For instance, if customers consistently lament about the poor quality of after-sales service in tech gadgets within your niche, there's a gap waiting to be filled.

By positioning your business to address these gaps, you create additional value for customers that competitors currently need to provide. This might mean offering more extended warranties, more responsive customer service, or more flexible product customization options than your competitors. By filling these gaps, you meet customer needs and position your business as a better alternative, turning market oversights into profitable opportunities. This approach attracts customers and builds a reputation for better understanding and meeting customer needs than anyone else in the market.

Sustainable Competitive Advantage: Building a sustainable competitive advantage that is hard to replicate.

A sustainable competitive advantage involves creating value that is not easily replicable by competitors. This might involve proprietary technology, a unique business model, or deep market insights. For example, if you've developed a software solution, investing in continuous technological improvements and patent protection can provide a durable competitive edge. Similarly, creating a brand synonymous with exceptional quality or customer service can turn customer loyalty into a competitive advantage.

Developing such an advantage often requires a combination of innovation, strategic foresight, and rigorous execution. It involves consistently staying ahead of industry trends, investing in research and development, and sometimes, making bold strategic decisions that may take time to pay off but will pave the way for long-term success. This enduring advantage can propel your business beyond sporadic success to become a dominant player in your industry.

Continuous Innovation: Continuous innovation is essential to maintain your competitive edge.

In today's fast-paced business world, resting on your laurels can be the quickest path to obsolescence. Continuous innovation is crucial not just for growth but for survival. This doesn't necessarily mean constant radical changes, but it does mean regularly evaluating and refining your offerings, processes, and customer interactions. It involves curiosity about emerging trends, customer behaviors, and technological advancements.

An effective way to embed continuous innovation into your business is to foster a culture that values creativity and experimentation. Encourage your team to bring new ideas, regardless of how unconventional they may seem. Implement systems that allow for quick testing of new concepts, whether a new marketing strategy or a product feature. Please solicit feedback from all stakeholders, including customers, employees, and partners, and use this feedback to make incremental improvements to your business.

By making innovation a core part of your business strategy, you ensure that your business adapts to changing market conditions and often stays ahead of them, securing your place at the forefront of your industry.

As we wrap up this chapter on validating your business idea, remember that this phase is about setting strong foundations and defining clear differentiators that set you apart in the marketplace. From understanding your unique selling proposition to leveraging competitive gaps, building sustainable advantages, and fostering continuous innovation, these strategies are designed to launch your business and propel it into a future of growth and success. As you move forward, keep refining these elements, and let them guide you in making strategic decisions that align with your vision and market realities.

In the next chapter, we will delve into the intricacies of effective business planning. These foundations will help you create a roadmap for your business that navigates through challenges and steers toward opportunities.

CHAPTER 3

MASTERING THE BASICS OF BUSINESS PLANNING

Imagine you are setting out to construct a house. Before even one brick is laid, you need a detailed blueprint—a clear plan guiding every construction step. Your business, too, requires such a blueprint: a robust business plan. This isn't just a document to attract investors; it's your roadmap, outlining how you'll navigate from the idea stage to a thriving enterprise. Whether you're pitching to investors, applying for loans, or guiding your team, a well-crafted business plan is indispensable. This chapter dives into building a bulletproof business plan that withstands scrutiny and guides your business with precision and adaptability.

3.1 THE ANATOMY OF A BULLETPROOF BUSINESS PLAN

Essential Components: Detailing the critical sections needed in every business plan.

A business plan should be a comprehensive guide, providing detailed information about your business model, market, goals, and more. At its core, every business plan should include several critical sections. First, an executive summary succinctly encapsulates your business concept, the problem it solves, your target market, and key financial highlights. Think of this as your elevator pitch in written form—it should be compelling enough to hook the reader's interest and encourage them to read further.

Next, delve into the business description, which offers a deeper look at your company and explains its nature and unique aspects. Follow this with a market analysis section, where you demonstrate your understanding of the industry, market trends, target audience, and competitive landscape. This section should reflect thorough research and present data to help you understand your assertions.

The organization and management section of your business plan outlines your company's structure and details the roles and responsibilities of your team members. This section is crucial, especially for potential investors, as it highlights the expertise and capabilities of your leadership team.

Another vital component is your service or product line section, where you describe your product or service, emphasizing customer benefits and the product lifecycle. Follow this up with marketing and sales strategies, showcasing how you intend to attract and retain customers and your sales process.

Lastly, the financial projections section is where you convince the reader that your business is a viable investment. Include detailed forecasts for income, cash flow, and balance sheets. Supplement these with a break-even analysis to show when your business will likely start turning a profit.

Tailoring for Your Audience: Customizing the plan for potential investors, lenders, or partners.

While the core components of your business plan are fundamental, the presentation might vary depending on the audience. For investors, focus on potential returns on investment, using market data and financial projections to build a compelling case. Highlight past achievements and future growth potential, and be ready to present scenarios that show how investment can accelerate growth.

For lenders, such as banks, the emphasis should be on the solidity of your financials and the viability of your business model. Lenders are primarily concerned with your ability to repay the loan, so include detailed, conservative financial forecasts and risk analysis. Demonstrating a thorough understanding of cash flow management is crucial here.

If your audience includes potential business partners, the business plan should detail the mutual benefits of the partnership. Focus on the synergy between the companies and how the partnership can foster growth, expand market reach, or increase product offerings.

Clarity and Conciseness: Keep your business plan concise and compelling.

Clarity and conciseness are paramount in any communication, and your business plan is no exception. Avoid jargon and complex terms that might obscure your message. Instead, use clear, straightforward language that makes your plan accessible to readers from various backgrounds. Each section should be concise yet packed with necessary information—think quality over quantity. The ability to distill complex concepts into digestible, engaging content is critical. This holds the reader's attention and ensures your business concepts are understood and remembered.

Iterative Process: View your business plan as a living document that evolves with your business.

A common misconception is that a business plan is a one-time document created at the start of a business and then left to gather dust. Your business plan should be a living document, regularly updated as your business evolves. This iterative process allows you to adapt to changes in the market environment, integrate new insights, and refine strategies as your business grows. Regularly revisiting and revising your business plan can help you stay aligned with your long-term goals while remaining flexible enough to capitalize on new opportunities. You can make it a routine part of your business review sessions, updating projections, milestones, and strategies to reflect current realities.

This dynamic approach to business planning ensures that your strategies remain relevant and robust, guiding your business through growth and change. As you move forward, keep these principles in mind. Your business plan is not just a tool for securing funding; it's a roadmap for your business's future, a document that evolves and adapts, just like your business. Use it to navigate the complexities of entrepreneurship, making informed decisions that drive sustainable growth.

3.2 FINANCIAL FORECASTING FOR THE NON-FINANCIAL FOUNDER

Navigating the financial aspects of running a business can often feel like steering a ship in foggy weather, especially if you need to become a finance expert. However, understanding basic financial concepts is crucial to keeping your business afloat and ensuring it thrives. Let's break down these concepts into manageable parts to help you feel more confident about your business's financial health.

Firstly, it's essential to grasp the basics: revenue, expenses, profits, and cash flow. Revenue is the money your business earns from normal business operations, calculated before any costs are deducted. Expenses are the costs incurred in the process of generating revenue. This includes costs like rent, salaries, and marketing. Profit, or net income, remains after all your business expenses have been subtracted from your total revenue. Understanding these terms is crucial because they reflect the financial health of your business at a fundamental level. Lastly, cash flow, which is the net amount of cash being transferred in and out of your business, is vital. It's possible to be profitable yet still struggle if your cash inflow doesn't match the timing of your outflows.

Creating realistic and defensible financial projections is your next step. This process involves estimating future sales, costs, and expenses to predict these economic outcomes. Start by examining historical data if available, and consider factors like market trends, your business growth stage, and seasonal fluctuations in your industry. When projecting sales, be conservative. Over-optimistic sales forecasts can lead to spending money you don't have, putting your business at risk. For expenses, it's safer to overestimate. This ensures you're prepared for unexpected costs, which are typical in most business operations. Remember, these projections are about predicting the future and preparing for it. They help you make informed decisions, like whether you can afford to hire new staff or upgrade your equipment.

Numerous tools and resources are available to streamline financial planning and simplify these tasks. Software like QuickBooks, Xero, and FreshBooks offers comprehensive accounting solutions to help you manage your books, from payroll to tax filing. These tools often come with user-friendly dashboards that provide at-a-glance insights into your financial status, helping you make quick decisions based on current data. Additionally, templates for financial projections are widely available online. These can be particularly useful for setting up your initial forecasts, as they typically come pre-filled with standard industry data, which you can customize for your specific needs.

Finally, interpreting financial data is a critical skill you must develop. This involves looking beyond the numbers to understand what they mean for your business. For instance, if your profit margins are declining, it could be a sign that your costs are rising or that you need to adjust your pricing strategy. Regularly reviewing financial statements like your balance sheet, income statement, and cash flow statement can provide insights into your business's economic health. The balance sheet gives a snapshot of your company's financial standing at a specific time, showing what you own (assets) versus what you owe (liabilities). The income statement (profit and loss) shows your revenues, costs, and expenses over time. This is crucial for understanding whether your business is operating at a profit or loss. The cash flow state-ment breaks down the cash inflow and outflow within your operations, investments, and financial activities, highlighting how money moves in and out of your business.

Managing these financial elements effectively ensures that your business stays solvent and capitalizes on opportunities to grow and expand. By taking the time to understand and implement these financial practices, you equip yourself with the knowledge to make informed decisions that enhance your business's capacity for success.

3.3 SETTING MILESTONES AND MEASURING SUCCESS

Creating a roadmap for your business with clearly defined milestones is akin to plotting waypoints on a long journey. These milestones serve as specific, measurable objectives that guide your business toward its long-term goals and provide a mechanism to gauge your progress. Setting these milestones begins with a deep understanding of your business objectives and breaking these down into smaller, achievable targets. For instance, if your ultimate goal is to expand your business nationally, your initial milestones include establishing a local customer base, then regional, before going national. Each phase should have a clear set of actions and a timeline. This systematic breakdown makes the goal seem more attainable and keeps your team focused and aligned.

When defining these milestones, it is crucial to ensure they are realistic and time-bound. A common pitfall for many new entrepreneurs is setting overly ambitious milestones without considering practical constraints like resource availability, market conditions, and operational capabilities. To avoid this, engage in thorough planning sessions with your team, utilize market data, and perhaps most importantly, learn from the experiences of others in your industry. Tools like Gantt charts can be highly effective in planning the timelines for each milestone, helping you visualize the sequence of activities that need to be completed and by when.

Once your milestones are set, the next step is to determine how you will measure success. This is where Key Performance Indicators (KPIs) come into play. KPIs are quantifiable measurements that reflect the critical success factors of a business. For a startup, these could include metrics like customer acquisition cost, customer retention rates, operational efficiency, or financial ratios like cash flow margin or return on investment. The key is to select KPIs that directly reflect the health of your business and align closely with your business goals. For example, if a milestone involves boosting production capacity, relevant KPIs might include production volume per week or manufacturing downtime.

KPIs not only help in measuring the effectiveness of your strategies but also provide insights that can lead to informed decision-making. For instance, if you notice that the customer acquisition cost is consistently higher than the industry average, it might indicate that your marketing strategies need refinement or that your sales funnel could be more efficient. Regularly reviewing these KPIs lets you stay on top of your business's performance and identify areas requiring attention or adjustment.

Adapting to feedback is crucial in the dynamic world of business. As you reach or approach each milestone, take the time to gather feedback—both from within your organization and external stakeholders like customers or partners. This feedback can provide valuable insights into how your business is perceived and areas where it can improve. For example, customer feedback on a new product launch can tell you what features are most appreciated and what aspects might need tweaking. Incorporating this feedback into your operations improves your product and enhances customer satisfaction and loyalty.

Celebrating success is as important as setting goals and measuring outcomes. Recognizing and celebrating each milestone boosts morale and fosters a culture of appreciation and success within your team. Whether it's a small get-together, a public acknowledgment, or a team outing, celebrating achievements can significantly enhance team cohesion and motivation. It reinforces the value of everyone's hard work and dedication towards achieving common goals. This practice keeps the team motivated and deeply ingrained in the company's journey toward success.

Setting clear, achievable milestones with associated KPIs helps systematically drive your business towards its objectives. Regularly reviewing these milestones and adapting your strategies based on real-world feedback ensures that your business remains flexible and responsive to change. Celebrating these achievements fosters a positive and motivated organizational culture crucial for sustained success. As you continue navigating the complexities of building your business, let these milestones be your guideposts, ensuring you remain on the path to achieving your vision.

3.4 RISK MANAGEMENT STRATEGIES FOR NEW VENTURES

Navigating the unpredictable terrain of new business ventures demands a strategic approach to risk management. Recognizing potential pitfalls and preparing appropriately can be the difference between thriving and faltering under pressure. The first step in effective risk management is identifying potential risks. This involves comprehensively analyzing internal and external factors that could impact your business. Internally, consider operational inefficiencies, employee turnover, or technological failures. Externally, look at market fluctuations, regulatory changes, or supply chain disruptions. Conducting a thorough risk assessment involves engaging with various stakeholders, including your management team, employees, and sometimes customers, to gain diverse perspectives on potential vulnerabilities. Tools such as SWOT analysis (Strengths, Weaknesses, Opportunities, Threats) can facilitate this process by structuring how you examine potential risks from all angles of your business operations.

Once risks are identified, the next critical step is to develop a risk management plan. This plan outlines how you plan to handle the risks you've identified, prioritizing them based on their likelihood and potential impact on your business. Strategies must be considered to avoid high-probability, high-impact risks entirely. For others, mitigating the risk by reducing the possibility of its occurrence or lessening its impact should it materialize is more viable. For instance, if data loss is a significant risk for your tech startup, investing in robust cybersecurity measures and regular data backups can mitigate this risk. The plan should also designate clear roles and responsibilities for risk management within your organization, ensuring everyone knows what to do if a particular risk becomes a reality. This structured approach prepares your business to handle crises more effectively and builds stakeholder confidence, showing you are proactive about safeguarding your venture.

Understanding the role of insurance and legal protection forms a cornerstone of any risk management strategy. Various types of business insurance exist to cover different risks, from general liability insurance that protects against legal hassles due to accidents, injuries, or negligence claims to product liability insurance in case your product causes harm to a user. Deciding on the right type and amount of insurance requires a clear understanding of the risks your business faces and the potential financial impact of those risks. Legal protection is equally crucial. This involves ensuring all aspects of your business align with legal requirements, from employment law to contract law and intellectual property rights. Consulting with legal professionals to ensure that your business complies with all applicable laws and regulations can prevent costly legal battles down the line. Moreover, understanding these legal intricacies can empower you to make informed decisions about your business operations, from hiring practices to marketing strategies and beyond.

Preparing for the unexpected with a solid crisis management plan is your final armor in risk management. Despite all efforts at risk identification and mitigation, it's possible to face unforeseen crises. A robust crisis management plan ensures you can respond immediately to such situations. This plan should include clear procedures for communication both internally within your organization and externally to customers, suppliers, and other stakeholders. It should detail the steps to address the crisis, who is responsible for each action, and how to escalate issues if necessary. Regularly reviewing and rehearsing this plan with your team can ensure that everyone knows how to act swiftly and efficiently, minimizing the impact of the crisis on your operations. This proactive preparation reflects strong leadership and a reliable commitment to your business's longevity, qualities that can stand your venture in good stead through turbulent times.

Incorporating these risk management strategies into your business planning process equips you with the knowledge and tools to anticipate potential challenges and react strategically, ensuring your business's resilience and sustainability. As you continue developing and refining these strategies, they become more than just a precaution—they evolve into a significant competitive advantage, enabling your business to navigate uncertainties confidently and quickly.

3.5 LEGAL ESSENTIALS: SETTING UP YOUR BUSINESS THE RIGHT WAY

Navigating the legal landscape of setting up a business is akin to learning a new language. It's detailed, often complex, and critical for ensuring your business operates smoothly and within the bounds of the law. A solid legal foundation protects your assets and intellectual property and builds credibility and trust with your customers, suppliers, and potential investors. Let's explore some fundamental legal essentials that are pivotal for every entrepreneur.

Choosing the proper business structure is one of the first and most important legal decisions you'll make. The structure you choose affects everything from your day-to-day operations, how much you pay in taxes, to the amount of your assets at risk. You can choose from several business structures, including sole proprietorship, partnership, corporation, S corporation, and Limited Liability Company (LLC). Each has its implications for liability, taxation, and operational complexity. For instance, a sole proprietorship is the simplest business entity, with no distinction between the business and the owner, making setup easy but exposing the owner to personal liability. On the other hand, an LLC provides limited liability protection, meaning personal assets are generally protected from business debts and claims. Meanwhile, corporations are ideal for businesses planning to raise money through stock sales but involve more complex regulations and tax requirements. The size and type of your business, industry, and future goals should influence the decision.

Registering your business is a critical step to becoming a legally recognized entity. This process varies depending on local regulations but typically involves registering your business name, obtaining a tax identification number, and securing necessary business licenses and permits. Please start by selecting a unique business name that meets your state's business laws and then register it to prevent other businesses from using the same name. The tax identification number, or Employer Identification Number (EIN), is essential for necessary steps like opening a business bank account and hiring employees. It's akin to a social security number for your business and can be obtained from the IRS. Depending on your business type and location, you may also need specific licenses and permits to operate legally. This could range from a general business license from your city or county to specialized manufacturing, transportation, and health services permits. The key here is to ensure full compliance to avoid legal complications that could derail your business operations.

Protecting your intellectual property (IP) is crucial in safeguarding the elements that set your business apart—unique products, services, or operational methods. IP protection involves securing your business' inventions, logos, original works, and design innovations. Depending on the IP, this can be achieved through patents, copyrights, trademarks, and trade secrets. For example, patents protect inventions and new processes, while trademarks protect brand identity elements like logos and slogans. Copyrights protect original works of authorship, including writings, music, and artworks. Considering the global marketplace, it's also wise to consider international protection if you sell products or services abroad. Early IP protection prevents others from profiting from your innovations and builds your business's asset base, potentially increasing its valuation.

Lastly, navigating the maze of required permits and regulatory compliance can seem daunting, but it is essential for operating your business without legal repercussions. This includes adhering to local, state, and federal regulations, which may involve everything from health and safety standards to environmental regulations. I'd like you to regularly review your compliance status and stay informed about changes in laws that could affect your industry. Compliance is not just about adhering to laws; it's about demonstrating your commitment to lawful and ethical business practices, which can significantly enhance your reputation and competitiveness.

Each aspect—from choosing the proper business structure to ensuring compliance with laws—is a pillar in building a legally sound business. While the initial effort might seem substantial, setting up your business legally protects it from potential risks and lays a robust foundation for future growth and success.

As we close this chapter on the legal essentials of setting up your business, remember that these steps are not mere formalities but crucial for building a resilient, compliant, and respected company. Your business is better equipped to navigate challenges and seize opportunities with the proper legal framework. Next, we will explore the exciting journey of financing your dream, where we will delve into various funding options and financial strategies to fuel your business growth.

CHAPTER 4

FINANCING YOUR DREAM

Starting your own business feels like standing at the base of a towering mountain. It's thrilling, yes, but undeniably daunting. The financial aspect of entrepreneurship often feels like the steepest part of the ascent. How you fund your venture can influence your business growth trajectory and the control you maintain over your creation. This chapter is dedicated to exploring the various paths you can take to finance your dream, starting with one of the most empowering yet challenging routes: boot-strapping.

4.1 BOOTSTRAPPING YOUR BUSINESS: A REALISTIC APPROACH

Bootstrapping is simple yet profound: it involves starting and growing your business using your resources without external funding. This approach isn't just about keeping your purse strings tight; it's a testament to your commitment and belief in your business concept, proving that you can do a lot with a little. Let's delve deeper into why bootstrapping could be a wise choice and how to effectively manage this approach to lay a solid foundation for your business.

Self-Funding Advantages: Understanding the benefits of bootstrapping your business.

Bootstrapping offers a distinct advantage by keeping you in complete control of your business decisions. Without investors to answer to, you can experiment and grow your business at your own pace based on what you believe is best. This autonomy is invaluable, especially in the early stages of fine-tuning your business model. Moreover, bootstrapping teaches you to be resourceful and innovative, qualities that define successful entrepreneurs. It forces you to think creatively, often leading to unique solutions that set your business apart from competitors who may be flush with cash but need more motivation to push boundaries. Additionally, funding your business from personal savings or revenue builds credibility and confidence among potential customers and partners. They see a business owner who is fully invested and believes in their venture enough to risk their funds, which can be a powerful statement in the business world.

Effective Cash Flow Management: Strategies for managing your finances when self-funding.

Managing cash flow effectively is critical when using your money to fund your business. It involves meticulous planning and continuous monitoring of how money is spent and earned. You can start by creating a detailed budget that outlines expected income and expenditures. This budget should be revisited and adjusted regularly as you gain more insight into your business's financial patterns. Prioritize expenditures that directly contribute to revenue generation while keeping overhead costs as low as possible. For instance, consider a co-working space or working from home instead of leasing a large office space. Additionally, quicken your receivables wherever possible. This might mean offering incentives for early payments or setting shorter payment terms for your clients. Keeping the cash flowing into the business is as crucial as managing the money going out.

Creative Cost-Cutting: Innovative ways to minimize expenses without sacrificing quality.

Finding innovative ways to minimize costs can significantly extend your runway when every dollar counts. You can start by scrutinizing every expense line to see where you can cut back without compromising the quality your customers expect. For example, consider freelancers or part-time workers instead of hiring full-time employees for roles that don't require full-time hours—leverage technology to automate tasks where possible, reducing the need for additional personnel. Negotiate with suppliers for better rates or find alternative suppliers offering competitive prices at the same or better quality. Another effective strategy is to barter services with other businesses. If you're a web design startup, you might offer your design services to a local attorney in exchange for legal advice. These creative strategies reduce costs and keep your business lean and flexible, allowing you to adapt quickly as your business grows.

Reinvesting Profits: The importance of reinvesting profits to fuel growth.

As your business starts to generate profit, it might be tempting to take it as personal earnings, especially if you've been tightening your belt for a while. However, reinvesting these profits into the business can significantly accelerate your growth. This reinvestment might mean expanding your product line, increasing your marketing budget to reach new customers, or investing in technology that improves operational efficiency. By continually reinvesting in your business, you build a stronger, more competitive company that can sustain long-term growth. This strategy also shows potential investors and partners that you are committed to expanding your business, which can be advantageous if you seek external funding.

Bootstrapping is not just a funding strategy; it's a mindset that challenges you to think differently, act resourcefully, and grow organically. It's about making smart decisions that keep your business agile and responsive to opportunities. As you leverage your resources to fuel your business journey, remember that each challenge is an opportunity to innovate, and each success is a testament to your dedication and entrepreneurial spirit. Keep pushing forward, optimizing, and letting your business's growth reflect your passion and perseverance.

4.2 NAVIGATING THE WORLD OF ANGEL INVESTORS AND VCS

Understanding the distinction between angel investors and venture capitalists (VCs) is crucial when considering external funding sources to elevate your business. Both types of investors can inject significant capital into your business, but their investment philosophies, expectations, and involvement levels differ markedly. Angel investors are typically affluent individuals who invest their money in startups at earlier stages, often for reasons beyond pure financial return, such as personal interest or a desire to mentor new entrepreneurs. They might be more flexible regarding investment terms and are often less aggressive about quick returns than venture capitalists. VCs, however, invest money from a professionally managed fund and tend to get involved with businesses that have proven their model but need capital to scale. They usually demand more control, often including a seat on the board, and have higher expectations for growth and returns.

Preparing for a pitch to these investors is more than just about having a good business idea. It's about articulating a clear vision, demonstrating deep market understanding, and showcasing a capable team to execute the business plan. Your pitch should succinctly answer why your business exists, what unique problem it solves, how significant the market opportunity is, and why you and your team are the ones to bring this idea to fruition. Financial projections should be realistic and backed by data. Be ready to dive deep into your business model, revenue streams, and growth strategy. Remember, investors are not just investing in your idea but in you as a leader. They need to believe in your capability to pivot and adapt, not just when things are going well, but more importantly, when they are not.

The decision to give away equity in your business is monumental. Equity financing means you are sharing a piece of your business's future. Every percentage point of equity you give away is a slice of your company's potential future profits and decision-making authority. Understand the implications of diluting your ownership. More investors mean potentially more people to answer to and more interests to serve, which might not always align with yours. It's crucial to think long-term. How much control are you willing to give up? What is the investor bringing to the table besides money? Can this partner open doors, provide expertise, and add value beyond capital? These questions can help you gauge whether giving up equity could be a worthwhile trade-off for accelerating your business's growth.

Building and maintaining relationships with investors goes beyond the initial pitch and investment phase. These relationships can be pivotal to your business's long-term success. Communication is key. Regular updates on your business's progress, challenges, and successes keep investors in the loop. Be transparent, especially when things don't go as planned. Investors can be invaluable advisors during tough times, offering guidance based on their experience and network. Additionally, respecting investors' insights and showing openness to feedback can fortify trust and respect. Investors are more likely to provide additional funding or support during subsequent rounds if they feel engaged and appreciated in the ongoing business journey. This relationship, nurtured with care, can significantly impact your current venture and potentially others.

Navigating the complex waters of equity financing requires a blend of strategic thinking, meticulous planning, and interpersonal skills. By understanding the different dynamics that angel investors and VCs bring, preparing thoroughly for your engagements with them, thoughtfully considering the equity you are willing to offer, and continuously nurturing these relationships, you set a solid foundation for not just securing funding but also building enduring partnerships that foster long-term business growth.

4.3 CROWDFUNDING STRATEGIES THAT WORK

In today's interconnected world, crowdfunding has emerged as a vibrant and viable method for raising funds, turning the traditional financing concept on its head. Instead of seeking out a few large investors, crowdfunding allows you to reach out to many potential backers who each contribute a small amount toward your project. The key to a successful crowdfunding campaign lies in what you are offering and how you engage with this expansive online community.

Choosing the Right Platform: Evaluating different crowdfunding platforms to find the best fit for your project.

The choice of platform can significantly influence the success of your crowdfunding campaign. Each platform comes with its own set of rules, target audience, and fee structures, making some better suited for certain types of projects than others. Kickstarter and Indiegogo, for example, are great for creative projects like tech gadgets, films, and art installations, often offering a rewards-based system where backers receive a product or a token of appreciation in return for their contribution. On the other hand, platforms like GoFundMe are better suited for personal fundraising and charitable causes. When selecting a platform, consider your project type, the audience you aim to attract, and the costs associated with using the platform. Assess how the platform's payment processing works, what happens to funds if the campaign doesn't reach its goal, and what support and tools are available to help you manage your campaign. Choosing the right platform sets the stage, but your campaign strategy ultimately determines whether the curtain calls on a successful funding round.

Crafting a Compelling Campaign: Key elements of a successful crowdfunding campaign.

The heart of a successful crowdfunding campaign is a compelling narrative. People connect with stories, not just ideas. Your campaign should tell a story that resonates with potential backers, making them feel a part of something larger than themselves. Start with a concise description of your project and why it matters. Be transparent about how the funds will be used and what milestones you aim to achieve. High-quality images and videos can significantly enhance your campaign's appeal, providing a visual connection to your narrative and helping backers feel more engaged with your project. It's also crucial to set realistic funding goals. Goals that are too high may not be met, which can be disheartening and may prevent you from keeping any of the funds, depending on the platform's policies. On the other hand, goals that are too low may need more capital to complete your project. Striking the right balance is critical, and it often helps to break down the budget so potential backers can see precisely where their money is going.

Engaging Your Audience: Strategies for building a community and engaging potential backers.

Building a community around your crowdfunding campaign can lead to more than just financial backing; it can create a group of ambassadors who believe in your mission and will spread the word to their networks. Engagement begins long before the campaign goes live.

Build momentum through your existing networks, including friends, family, and professional contacts. Utilize social media platforms to start conversations around your project's themes and share progress updates and behind-the-scenes content to keep your audience engaged and invested in the journey. Regular updates throughout the campaign can help maintain momentum, keeping backers informed and engaged. Additionally, prompt responses to questions or comments publicly on the crowdfunding platform and privately via emails or direct messages show that you value your backers' interest and support, fostering a stronger connection.

Post-Campaign Follow-up: Maintaining momentum and fulfilling promises after the campaign ends.

Once your crowdfunding campaign has concluded successfully, the real work begins. It's crucial to maintain the trust and support of your backers through transparent and ongoing communication. Start by thanking your backers promptly and providing a clear timeline for the project's next steps. Regular updates on the progress of the project, challenges encountered, and milestones reached keep backers informed and engaged. If delays or issues arise, communicate these openly and explain what actions are being taken to address them. Fulfilling rewards or promises to backers as soon as possible is a matter of responsibility and helps build a lasting relationship with your community. This ongoing engagement and fulfillment of pledges reinforce the trust backers have in you, potentially making them more likely to support your future projects.

Navigating the world of crowdfunding requires a blend of storytelling, strategic planning, community engagement, and meticulous follow-through. By effectively leveraging the power of the crowd, you can secure the funding needed to bring your business dreams to life and build a foundation of supporters who are invested in your success far beyond the financial contributions they make. As you embark on this funding path, remember that the relationships you build and the community you cultivate can become one of your venture's most valuable assets, enduring well beyond the campaign itself.

4.4 GRANT OPPORTUNITIES AND HOW TO APPLY

Exploring grant opportunities can open doors to funding that doesn't need to be repaid, making it an alluring option for any business owner eager to find financial support without diluting their equity or accumulating debt. Government entities, non-profit organizations, and private foundations typically offer grants, each with its own goals and criteria. To tap into this resource, a clear understanding of how to navigate the grant landscape is crucial.

Finding Grants: How to find grant opportunities relevant to your business.

Finding grants can seem like searching for needles in a haystack if you don't know where to look. Begin by identifying which type of grants you are eligible for based on your industry, business size, and specific needs such as research and development, technology upgrades, or expansion. Utilize government databases such as Grants.gov in the United States, which offers a centralized location for grant seekers to find and apply for federal funding opportunities. Please expand your search to include state and local government grants and grants offered by corporations and non-profit organizations that align with your business goals. Industry-specific grants can also be particularly beneficial. For instance, if your business focuses on environmental sustainability, seek grants to promote green technologies or sustainable practices.

Networking with other business owners and attending industry conferences can also provide leads on grant opportunities that may be less widely advertised.

Eligibility and Requirements: Understanding grant eligibility and application requirements.

Each grant has its own set of eligibility criteria and application requirements. These can range from the geographical location and the size of your business to specific demographic factors like minority-owned businesses or female entrepreneurship. Before you go through the application process, please review these criteria to ensure you meet all the requirements. This not only saves time but also increases your chances of success. Please pay close attention to the documentation needed for the application. Typical requirements include a detailed business plan, financial statements, tax returns, and a clear explanation of how the grant money will be used. Some grants may also require specific certifications or proof of particular achievements, such as environmental compliance certificates or quality standards awards.

Writing a Winning Proposal: Tips for writing a compelling grant proposal.

Your grant proposal is your pitch to the grantor, and it needs to make a compelling case for why your business deserves the funding. You can start with a concise executive summary outlining what your company does, why the grant money is needed, and how it will make a difference. This section should grab the reader's attention and make them want to read more. In the main body of the proposal, detail your business's objectives, the problem you're solving, and the specific outcomes you expect to achieve with the grant funding. Use data and specific examples to strengthen your case and align your goals with the grantor's objectives.

For instance, if the grant aims to boost local employment, detail how the funds will enable you to hire locally. Be clear and precise in your writing, avoiding jargon and technical terms that might obscure your message. Finally, your proposal should include a detailed budget that itemizes how every dollar of the grant will be spent, demonstrating your thoughtful and strategic approach to finances.

Managing Grant Funds: Best practices for managing grant funds effectively if awarded.

Receiving a grant is only the beginning. Proper management of the funds is critical to meet the project's objectives and comply with the grantor's expectations. Establish a separate bank account for the grant money to ensure that funds are used only for grant-related activities. This separation also simplifies accounting and auditing processes. Develop a detailed financial plan that aligns with the budget submitted in your grant proposal. Regularly review your expenditures against this budget and adjust as necessary to stay on track. Documentation is critical; keep detailed records of all expenses, including receipts, invoices, and bank statements. These records will be invaluable during periodic reporting to the grantor, where you'll need to demonstrate that the funds have been used appropriately and effectively. Additionally, regular internal or external audits should be considered to ensure compliance with grant usage and identify any improvement areas in financial management.

Grants provide a unique opportunity for business funding, as they do not require repayment. This makes them a desirable option for business owners looking to expand or innovate without increasing their debt load. By understanding how to find and apply for grants, writing a compelling proposal, and managing the funds effectively, you can maximize this funding source's benefits, helping propel your business toward its strategic goals.

As we conclude this chapter, remember that funding your business dream involves exploring various avenues and leveraging every opportunity. Grants are just one part of a broader financial strategy that may also include bootstrapping, seeking investors, and crowdfunding. Each method has strengths and challenges; the correct mix will depend on your business needs, goals, and context. In the next chapter, we will focus on establishing a compelling brand, a critical component in ensuring that your well-funded business effectively captures and retains the attention of its target audience.

CHAPTER 5

ESTABLISHING A COMPELLING BRAND CAPTURED AND EXPANDED

In the vibrant mosaic of the marketplace, your brand is your distinct hue, your unique brushstroke that sets you apart from the myriad of other colors blending into the background. Think of your brand as your business's personality, its voice, and its promise to your customers— it's what they come to trust and, ultimately, remain loyal to. Starting your journey with a strong branding strategy isn't just about having a memorable logo or an attractive color scheme; it's about creating an identity that resonates deeply with your target audience, compelling them to choose you over your competitors. Whether you are crafting this identity from scratch or refining an existing one, the essence of effective branding lies in consistency and engagement. Let's explore how you, as an entrepreneur, can craft a compelling brand on a budget, using creative strategies and tools to save costs and carve a distinct niche in the competitive market landscape.

5.1 BRANDING ON A BUDGET: DIY STRATEGIES FOR STARTUPS

Leveraging Free Tools: Identifying and utilizing free or low-cost branding tools efficiently

In the digital age, various free and low-cost tools can help you establish a professional-looking brand without necessitating a hefty investment. Tools like Canva offer user-friendly design templates for everything from logos to business cards and social media posts, allowing you to maintain a sleek, consistent aesthetic across all your branding materials. For website development, platforms such as WordPress and Wix provide customizable templates tailored to suit your brand's look and feel without extensive coding knowledge. Google's suite of tools, including Analytics for tracking website performance and Trends for understanding consumer search behaviors, can also be invaluable in refining your branding strategy based on actual data. By smartly utilizing these tools, you can create a cohesive and attractive brand presence that speaks directly to your target audience, enhancing your business's credibility and appeal.

Creative Branding Techniques: Innovative techniques to create a memorable brand identity without a hefty price tag

Creativity in branding isn't about how much money you can spend but how effectively you can communicate your brand's story and values. One impactful technique is storytelling to forge a deeper connection with your audience. Share the genesis story of your business, the challenges you've overcome, and the milestones you've achieved. This narrative can be woven into all your communications, from your website's about page to your social media posts, making your brand feel more relatable and inspiring. Another technique is guerrilla marketing—unconventional, low-cost marketing tactics that can generate significant public interest.

For example, if you're launching a health food café, a pop-up stand in local community events offering free samples of your signature dishes can create buzz and attract potential customers. Such creative endeavors can set your brand apart and generate word-of-mouth, amplifying your brand's presence in the market.

Community Engagement: Building your brand through active community engagement and participation

Your brand's strength is significantly bolstered by the community you build around it. Engaging with your community doesn't have to be costly. It can be as simple as participating in local events or hosting workshops that reflect your brand's mission. For instance, if your brand promotes eco-friendly products, organizing community clean-up days or educational talks on sustainability can reinforce your brand's values and enhance its visibility and relevance. Online, this engagement can extend to actively conversing with followers on social media, running contests, or creating interactive content that encourages participation. Each interaction is an opportunity to demonstrate your brand's commitment to its customers and values, fostering a loyal community that grows with your brand.

Brand Consistency: Ensuring brand consistency across all platforms and materials on a budget

The cornerstone of effective branding is consistency; your brand should be immediately recognizable, whether seen on a billboard, a web page, or a product packaging. This consistency extends beyond visual elements like logos and color schemes to include the tone of voice used in your communications and the overall customer experience you provide. To ensure consistency, develop a brand style guide that outlines how your brand's elements should be used across various mediums. This guide should include specific details about your color palette, typography, imagery style, and key messaging points. It should also outline the voice and tone used in all communications, ensuring that your brand's personality is consistent whether you are tweeting, answering customer emails, or creating promotional materials. A well-defined style guide ensures that everyone in your organization and any external partners you work with can consistently apply your brand elements, reinforcing your brand's identity at every touchpoint.

In this digital era, where the barriers to entry are lower than ever, a strong brand can be the deciding factor in your business's success. You can build a brand that captures attention and wins hearts and minds by utilizing free tools, embracing creativity, engaging with your community, and maintaining consistency. Remember, your brand is more than just a logo or a slogan—it reflects your business's identity, values, and promise to your customers. Make it as compelling and authentic as possible, and watch as it becomes your most valuable asset in the bustling marketplace.

5.2 THE POWER OF STORYTELLING IN BUSINESS

Storytelling isn't just an art form; in the business context, it's a strategic tool that can significantly enhance your brand's appeal and customer retention. When you craft your brand's story, it's about weaving the facts of your products or services into a narrative that resonates with your audience on a deeper level. This narrative should encapsulate what you offer, why you do what you do, and the values that guide your operations. Think about your brand's origins, the challenges you've faced, and how they have shaped the vision of your business. For instance, if your company started in a small home kitchen and now delivers organic meals city-wide, your story isn't just about the meals but about a passion for healthy eating and local farming. This story should be compelling, making someone stop and think or feel inspired to act, fostering a deeper connection with your brand.

Creating this emotional connection is crucial. Emotions drive decisions. A brand that connects emotionally educates, entertains, or inspires always stands out. Consider how certain brands have made you feel, whether it's a sense of adventure, safety, or nostalgia. These feelings often influence buying decisions more than the actual features of a product. For your brand, identify the emotions that align with your business values and are likely to resonate with your target audience. Then, infuse these emotions into your storytelling. If your brand is about innovation and technology, your stories might evoke awe and wonder through tales of ingenuity and problem-solving. Every piece of content you create, every product you launch, and every interaction with customers should consistently reflect this emotional underpinning, making your brand seen and felt.

Choosing the right platforms to share your brand story is equally vital. Each platform offers different strengths and caters to other demographics. Your website is your brand's home, where the depth of your story can be explored. Blogs, about pages, and even your product descriptions are opportunities to tell your story.

Social media platforms, on the other hand, allow for more frequent and informal engagement. Video platforms like YouTube are excellent for storytelling through visual content, where you can create videos that show your products in action or feature customer testimonials that align with your brand narrative. Meanwhile, platforms like Instagram or Pinterest can be used to share visual snippets of your story, highlighting moments that capture the essence of your brand, from behind-the-scenes photos to customer stories. Choosing the right mix of platforms ensures that your story reaches your audience where they are most likely to engage with it.

Integrating your story across every customer touchpoint is the final piece of the puzzle. This integration means that from the first time a potential customer hears about your brand, through every stage of their interaction with your company, they should encounter aspects of your story. It could be through the tone and content of your emails, the design of your packaging, or the customer service they receive. For instance, if one of your brand stories is about commitment to customer satisfaction, reinforce this narrative by resolving customer issues quickly and effectively and follow up with a personalized thank you note. Such actions reaffirm your brand's narrative and build trust. In-store experiences, if applicable, should also reflect your brand's story through the store layout, the staff's behavior, and the information available about your products. Even in a digital age, physical touchpoints are potent conduits for storytelling.

Through thoughtful storytelling, you can transform your brand from just another choice in the market to a meaningful part of your customers' lives. Stories have the power to engage the mind and touch the heart, making them one of the most potent tools in your branding arsenal. As you continue to weave your brand's story into the fabric of your business, remember that consistency, emotional resonance, and strategic platform selection are crucial to creating a narrative that not only attracts but retains a loyal customer base.

5.3 DESIGNING YOUR VISUAL IDENTITY: LOGOS, COLORS, AND MORE

Creating a visual identity that truly stands out begins with a solid understanding of the fundamentals that make up your brand's visual language. This encompasses everything from the logo that marks your products or advertisements to the color schemes that paint your website and promotional materials. A strong visual identity is not just about being aesthetically pleasing—it's about being memorable, conveying your brand's values, and ensuring recognition across varied platforms. Your logo, for instance, is often the first encounter someone has with your brand. It should, therefore, be simple enough to be memorable but powerful enough to convey the essence of your brand. Please think of the Nike swoosh or the Apple apple; these logos are iconic in their simplicity and effectiveness in evoking recognition and the brand's ethos. To achieve this, start by sketching ideas that reflect your brand's core values and mission. It might be beneficial to involve your team in this brainstorming session, as multiple perspectives can spark creativity and lead to a more refined outcome.

In today's DIY era, the accessibility of design tools has revolutionized how startups approach creating their logos and branding materials. Platforms like Adobe Spark or LogoMakr provide user-friendly interfaces that allow even those with minimal graphic design experience to create professional-looking logos. These tools often come with pre-designed templates that can be customized to suit your brand's color scheme and typographic preferences. The key here is to experiment with different designs until you find one that feels right for your brand. Remember, your logo is a long-term investment. The design should resonate with your current business vision and be versatile enough to remain relevant as your business grows and evolves.

The psychology of color is pivotal in how your brand is perceived. Colors evoke emotions and can significantly impact consumer behavior. For example, blue often instills a sense of trust and reliability and is favored by financial institutions. Green, frequently associated with health and tranquility, is a favorite for organic and eco-friendly brands. When choosing colors for your brand, consider the emotions and messages you want to communicate. Tools like Coolors or Adobe Color can help you explore color palettes and their psychological impacts. Consistency in your color choice across all your branding materials reinforces brand recognition. If your logo is green and white, echoing these colors on your website, social media profiles, and even your business cards creates a cohesive visual experience for customers.

Ensuring your visual identity is consistently applied across all media and platforms is crucial for maintaining brand integrity. This consistency extends beyond using the same logo or color scheme; it involves aligning the style of your imagery, the tone of your visuals, and even the quality of your graphics across all touchpoints. Whether customers visit your website, receive an email, or see your advertisement on social media, they should immediately recognize your brand. To manage this, create a detailed brand style guide that outlines how and where each element of your visual identity should be used. This guide should provide clear instructions on logo placement, color palette usage, typography, imagery style, and even the tone of the visuals. By ensuring that everyone from your marketing team to external designers adheres to this guide, you maintain a cohesive and professional brand appearance that customers will recognize and trust over time.

Building a standout visual identity involves more than creating a logo or selecting colors. It's about crafting a visual language that communicates your brand's values, resonates with your target audience, and remains consistent across all platforms. Whether utilizing DIY design tools or exploring the psychology behind colors, each step contributes to a stronger, more cohesive brand identity that captures attention and fosters brand loyalty. As you continue to develop and refine your brand's visual elements, remember that each visual choice you make is an opportunity to strengthen your connection with your audience, making your brand not just seen but remembered.

5.4 CRAFTING YOUR ONLINE PRESENCE: WEBSITE AND SOCIAL MEDIA BASICS

In today's digital ecosystem, your online presence is often the first point of contact between your brand and potential customers. It is a virtual handshake—a crucial opportunity to make a lasting impression. Therefore, crafting a robust online presence through a well-designed website and strategic social media use is indispensable. A startup's website should be seen as a digital brochure and a dynamic platform that informs, engages, and converts visitors. Every startup website should clearly describe who you are and what your business offers right on the homepage. This immediate clarity helps potential customers understand your business without navigating multiple pages. Include an 'About Us' page that shares your business's story and values, connecting emotionally with visitors and giving a personal touch that can set you apart from competitors.

Next, please make sure that your website includes a straightforward way for customers to reach out to you. A 'Contact' page with multiple communication options such as phone, email, and perhaps a contact form, along with links to your business's social media platforms, ensures potential customers can reach you effortlessly. Moreover, integrating an FAQ section can be incredibly beneficial, as it addresses common customer queries and concerns, reducing the barrier to action, whether that action is making a purchase or signing up for a newsletter. Customer testimonials or case studies should also be featured to build trust and validate your business's credibility. These testimonials serve as social proof that your products or services deliver on their promises, reassuring potential customers they may need to decide.

Optimizing for user experience (UX) is critical in ensuring your website attracts visitors and keeps them engaged. The key to a user-friendly website is simplicity and speed. Please ensure your site has a clean, uncluttered design that is easy to navigate. A complicated layout can confuse visitors and increase their chances of abandoning your site. The website's loading speed is crucial; slow-loading pages can frustrate users and negatively impact search engine rankings. Tools like Google PageSpeed Insights can be used to check your website's speed and get specific recommendations for improvement. Responsive design is another critical factor in UX, ensuring your website looks good and functions well on all devices, from desktops to smartphones. With increasing users accessing the internet via mobile devices, a mobile-friendly website is essential to provide a seamless user experience.

Developing a cohesive social media strategy is another pillar in building a solid online presence. You can start by identifying which social media platforms are most popular with your target audience. Each platform has its culture and best practices; choosing the ones where your presence will be most beneficial is crucial. For instance, platforms like Instagram and Pinterest can be more effective if your business is highly visual. On the other hand, if your focus is more on professional networking or B2B sales, LinkedIn might be a better fit. Once you've selected your platforms, consistency is critical. Regular posting according to a schedule helps keep your audience engaged and your brand top-of-mind. Use a mix of content types, including images, videos, infographics, and text posts, to keep your content fresh and engaging. Each post should reflect your brand's voice and values, contributing to a consistent brand identity across platforms.

Content planning is vital in maintaining a consistent and engaging online presence. Developing a content calendar can help organize and schedule content for your website and social media platforms, ensuring regular updates without last-minute scrambles. This calendar should align with your business's promotional activities, such as product launches or seasonal sales, as well as relevant national or international days that resonate with your brand. For instance, an eco-friendly brand might focus on content around Earth Day. Content should be designed not only to inform and entertain but also to encourage interaction and sharing. Engaging content prompts keep your audience interested and increase the likelihood of them sharing your content, expanding your reach organically. Additionally, use analytics tools to track the performance of your content. This data can provide insights into what types of content your audience finds most engaging, allowing you to refine your strategy and focus more on what works, enhancing the effectiveness of your online communication.

In sum, your online presence, from your website's user experience to your social media content, plays a pivotal role in how your brand is perceived and interacted with in the digital world. As you continue to build and refine your online strategy, remember that each element, from website design to content creation, should be thoughtfully aligned with your brand's goals, providing a cohesive and engaging experience that converts visitors into loyal customers.

5.5 NETWORKING AND BUILDING STRATEGIC PARTNERSHIPS

Forging strategic partnerships and honing your networking skills can amplify your brand's reach and depth in the bustling business ecosystem. The process begins by identifying potential partners synergizing with your brand's values and goals. This alignment is crucial as it ensures that both parties work towards a common purpose, making the partnership more likely to succeed and be mutually beneficial. To identify these potential partners, start by analyzing your business's needs and how a partner could help meet these needs. For example, if your business is a startup focused on sustainable fashion, potential partners could include fabric suppliers committed to eco-friendly materials or retail stores specializing in sustainable products. Attending industry events, trade shows, and seminars can also provide opportunities to connect with potential partners. Additionally, leveraging online platforms like LinkedIn can help you research and connect with companies and key figures within your target partnership sphere.

Please don't hesitate to contact them as soon as you have identified potential partners. This initial contact should be thoughtful and personalized, demonstrating a clear understanding of the potential partner's business and how the partnership could benefit them. A well-crafted proposal outlining potential collaboration areas can make a significant impact. This proposal should include specific details on how the partnership can help achieve shared goals, backed by data or case studies highlighting potential benefits. It's also important to be flexible and open to feedback, as the initial proposal may evolve through discussions to better align with both parties' objectives and capabilities.

Beyond identifying and approaching potential partners, mastering the art of networking is essential for building and nurturing relationships that could lead to future partnerships. Effective networking is more than just exchanging business cards; it's about creating genuine connections and offering value. One effective strategy is to be a connector yourself, helping others in your network connect with potential partners, clients, or resources. This builds goodwill and establishes you as a valuable and influential figure within your industry. Additionally, consistently engaging with your network through follow-ups, sharing relevant information, or just checking in can keep relationships warm and top of mind, increasing the likelihood of collaborations in the future.

Exploring collaboration opportunities involves being creative and open to various forms of partnerships. These could range from co-branding efforts, where both brands come together for a joint product release, to more complex joint ventures, where resources are pooled to create a new entity or service. Each collaboration opportunity should be evaluated regarding strategic fit, potential market impact, and alignment with long-term goals. For instance, a temporary pop-up collaboration with a complementary brand can create buzz and reach new customer segments while testing the waters for more permanent collaborations.

Leveraging partnerships effectively is about maximizing each partner's strengths for mutual benefit. Clear communication, defined roles, and regular progress reviews can help ensure that all parties are aligned and that the partnership is on track to meet its objectives. Measuring the partnership's success through predefined metrics, such as increased brand exposure, sales uplift, or customer engagement metrics, is also essential. These insights can help refine future partnership strategies and demonstrate the value of strategic collaborations.

In summary, building strategic partnerships and honing networking skills are about more than just expanding your brand's reach; they are about creating opportunities for growth, innovation, and connection. By identifying the right partners, engaging effectively, exploring creative collaboration opportunities, and leveraging the strengths of each partnership, your brand can enhance its market presence and deepen its impact and relevance in the industry.

As we wrap up this chapter on establishing a compelling brand, we see how strategic partnerships and robust networking extend your brand's reach and enrich its narrative and community ties. These collaborations can open up new avenues for growth that you might have needed help to tap into. The next chapter will focus on smart marketing strategies for startups. Here, we will delve into how you can effectively market your brand to ensure your message resonates with and reaches your intended audience, turning potential customers into loyal advocates.

CHAPTER 6

SMART MARKETING FOR STARTUPS

Marketing your startup is not just about broadcasting your products or services to the world; it's about strategically connecting with your audience, engaging them in meaningful ways, and building lasting relationships that convert followers into customers and then into advocates. In this digital age, where every startup has access to the same online platforms, standing out requires more than just showing up. It demands a deep understanding of your audience, a creative approach to communication, and a consistent strategy that aligns with your brand values and business goals. Let's delve into the essentials of SEO and content marketing— beneficial and necessary tools for any startup looking to make its mark in the crowded online marketplace.

6.1 SEO AND CONTENT MARKETING ESSENTIALS

SEO Basics for Startups: Understanding the fundamentals of SEO and how it can drive organic traffic to your website.

Search Engine Optimization (SEO) is your golden ticket to organic visibility on the internet. At its core, SEO is about enhancing your website's presence in search engine results, making it easier for your target audience to discover you amidst a sea of competitors. Understanding SEO starts with recognizing its two main components: on-page SEO, which involves optimizing elements within your website like content, images, and HTML tags, and off-page SEO, which focuses on external factors like backlinks from other websites. Both are crucial in improving your website's credibility and ranking in search engine results. Implementing basic SEO strategies such as using relevant keywords, ensuring your website is mobile-friendly, optimizing your site's loading speed, and securing your site with HTTPS can significantly boost your visibility. Remember, the goal of SEO is not just to increase traffic but to attract the right kind of traffic that is likely to convert into leads and customers.

Content Creation Strategies: Develop a content strategy that boosts SEO and engages your target audience.

Content is the heart of any effective SEO strategy. However, creating content that engages your audience and boosts SEO rankings requires a strategic approach. Start by understanding the needs and preferences of your target audience. What information are they looking for? What problems do they need solutions to?

Once you have this insight, you can create content that meets their needs and interests, from blog posts and articles to videos and infographics. Each piece of content should be crafted with attention to SEO, incorporating keywords naturally and focusing on relevant topics for your audience. But remember, quality trumps quantity. It's better to publish one well-researched, well-written piece of content each week than to push out daily posts that don't add value to your audience. High-quality content keeps your audience coming back and establishes your brand as an authority in your field, which can enhance your SEO efforts.

Keyword Research: Conducting effective keyword research to guide your content creation efforts.

Keyword research is critical for any content strategy because it tells you what your target audience is searching for on search engines. Tools like Google's Keyword Planner or SEMrush can provide insights into the keywords related to your business with high search volumes and low competition. This research can guide your content creation, ensuring that you focus on topics that have actual demand. When integrating these keywords into your content, it's essential to do so naturally—forcing too many keywords into your text (a practice known as 'keyword stuffing') can hurt your SEO efforts. Instead, use keywords thoughtfully and sparingly to create informative and engaging content.

They are measuring SEO Success: Tools and metrics to measure the impact of your SEO and content marketing efforts.

Measuring the impact of your SEO and content marketing strategies is essential to understanding the effectiveness of your SEO and content marketing strategies. Tools like Google Analytics offer comprehensive insights into your website's traffic, including which pages attract the most visitors, how long visitors stay on your site, and what actions they take. These metrics can help you determine the quantity of your traffic and the quality—how engaged your visitors are and how likely they are to convert into customers. Other key metrics to track include your website's bounce rate, the number of inbound links from other reputable websites, and your ranking on search engine results pages for critical keywords. Regularly reviewing these metrics can help refine your strategies, enhancing your online presence and effectiveness.

Investing in SEO and content marketing can sometimes take a back seat to more immediate concerns like product development or sales in the whirlwind of starting a new business. However, these digital strategies are not just add-ons but crucial tools that can drive your business's long-term growth and success. By understanding and implementing the basics of SEO, developing a strategic content approach, conducting thorough keyword research, and regularly measuring the impact of your efforts, you can build a solid online presence that attracts, engages, and retains customers. As you continue through this chapter, remember that each tool and strategy you learn is about promoting your business, connecting with your audience in meaningful ways, building trust, and establishing a brand that stands out in today's competitive market.

6.2 LEVERAGING SOCIAL MEDIA FOR BUSINESS GROWTH

Navigating the vast landscape of social media can feel like steering a vessel in open waters—exciting yet daunting. The key lies in selecting the right platforms where your potential customers are most active and engaged. Each social media platform offers unique features and caters to specific demographics, making some more suitable than others for your business goals. For instance, if your target audience comprises young, creative individuals, platforms like Instagram and TikTok, known for their visual and video content, might be more effective. Conversely, LinkedIn could offer more value if you focus on professional networking or B2B sales. The best approach is to start by identifying where your target customers spend their time. Look at demographic data provided by each platform, consider the type of content that performs best on each, and evaluate how well these align with your marketing goals. Remember, being present on every platform is less important than being impactful on the right ones. Once you've selected your platforms, it's crucial to tailor your content and engagement strategies to fit each platform's unique culture and user expectations. This enhances your brand's appeal and increases the likelihood of engaging effectively with your audience.

Developing a social media calendar is an effective strategy to ensure a consistent and impactful online presence. This involves planning your posts, usually monthly or weekly, to maintain a steady flow of content that keeps your audience engaged and informed. You can start by identifying key dates relevant to your brand, such as product launches, promotional events, or significant holidays, and plan content around these. It's also helpful to establish a regular posting schedule that keeps your audience anticipating your content, whether "Tutorial Tuesdays" or "Feature Fridays." Additionally, incorporating various content types, such as videos, live streams, images, and polls, can keep your feed dynamic and exciting to your followers. Tools like Hootsuite or Buffer can be incredibly helpful in scheduling and managing posts across multiple platforms, allowing you to maintain an active social media presence without manually posting content daily. The goal of your content calendar should be to promote your products or services and tell your brand's story, share valuable information, and engage in conversations that matter to your audience, helping to build a community around your brand.

The effectiveness of your social media efforts hinges not just on promotion but on engagement. While informing your audience about your offerings is essential, focusing too much on self-promotion can turn followers off. Instead, prioritize content that engages your audience in meaningful ways. Ask questions, share helpful tips, respond to comments, and participate in trends that resonate with your brand. This approach fosters a stronger connection with your audience and encourages more interaction, boosting your visibility on social media algorithms. For example, you might run a weekly Q&A session where you address customer questions live or create interactive stories where followers can vote on their favorite products. Remember, social media is a two-way street; the more you engage with your audience, the more likely they are to engage with your content, enhancing your brand's presence and appeal online.

Lastly, tracking and utilizing analytics is crucial in refining your social media strategy and increasing engagement. Most social media platforms provide built-in analytics tools that allow you to track various metrics such as engagement rates, reach, impressions, and click-through rates. Regularly reviewing these metrics lets you gain valuable insights into what types of content perform best, what times your audience is most active, and how they interact with your content. This data can help you fine-tune your strategy, focusing more on what works and less on what doesn't. Additionally, social media analytics can provide deeper insights into your audience's demographics and preferences, informing your social media strategy and broader marketing and product development strategies. For instance, if you notice that a particular type of post consistently yields high engagement, you might consider using similar themes or formats in your more extensive marketing campaigns or even developing new product features that align with audience preferences.

By strategically choosing the right platforms, creating a structured content calendar, focusing on engagement over promotion, and utilizing analytics to refine your approach, you can leverage social media to market your business and grow it. With each post, you can reach new eyes and connect with hearts and minds, building a community that supports and sustains your company in the ever-evolving digital landscape.

6.3 EMAIL MARKETING STRATEGIES FOR ENGAGEMENT AND CONVERSION

The digital landscape is bustling with myriad marketing tactics, yet email marketing remains a cornerstone strategy for its direct approach and personal touch. Building a robust email list from scratch is akin to laying the foundation for a house; it must be done with precision and foresight, ensuring it supports the structure—your marketing campaigns—that will eventually stand on it. Start by leveraging every touchpoint where potential subscribers interact with your brand. This could be on your website, during checkout processes, or at physical locations with signage encouraging customers to sign up. Offer incentives that add value, such as exclusive discounts, early access to products, or insightful newsletters. Remember, the key is to offer something compelling enough that a visitor is willing to exchange their email for it. Tools like pop-up forms integrated into your website can be effective, especially when timed to appear after someone has engaged with your content for a particular duration. Ensuring that the sign-up process is as straightforward as possible, a complicated process can deter potential subscribers. Additionally, always adhere to legal standards like GDPR to build trust with your subscribers; let them know their data is safe.

I want you to know that crafting compelling emails that engage and convert begins with understanding the interests and needs of your audience. Every email should have a clear purpose aligning with your audience's expectations and business goals. The content should be relevant and provide value, whether a promotional email about a new product or a monthly newsletter. This could be through insightful information, entertainment, or special offers. The subject line is your first impression and, often, the make-or-break point that determines whether an email is opened. Make it catchy but not misleading, and align it with the content of your email. The body of your email should maintain this engagement, using a friendly and conversational tone that resonates with your audience. Visual elements like images and videos can enhance the appeal, but they should not overshadow the message. A clear call-to-action (CTA) should be evident, guiding recipients on what to do next, whether visiting a landing page, purchasing, or another step. Remember, every email is a step towards building a stronger relationship with your customer, so personal touches can make a significant difference.

Segmentation and personalization are techniques that transform generic email blasts into targeted messages that speak directly to the recipient, significantly increasing engagement and conversion rates. Segmentation involves dividing your email list into smaller segments based on specific criteria such as purchase history, geographic location, or behavior. This allows you to tailor your messages to each segment's interests and needs. For example, sending a special offer on winter wear to customers in colder regions can see better engagement compared to sending this same offer to everyone on your list. Personalization goes further by tailoring the email to individual preferences and behaviors. This could be as simple as including the recipient's name in the email or as complex as recommending products based on their browsing history on your site. Data is critical in personalization; the more you know about your subscribers, the more tailored your emails can be. This approach enhances the relevancy of your messages and strengthens the relationship with your customers, making them feel valued and understood.

A/B testing, or split testing, is critical in refining your email marketing to ensure maximum effectiveness. This involves sending two variations of the same email to a small percentage of your mailing list to see which version performs better. You can test subject lines, email content, CTA buttons, or sending times. The results can provide valuable insights that can be used to optimize your entire email marketing strategy. For instance, discovering that emails sent on a Tuesday morning have higher open rates than those sent on Friday evenings can help you time your emails better.

Similarly, finding that emails with personalized subject lines perform better can encourage you to adopt personalization more broadly in your campaigns. Regular A/B testing keeps your strategies fresh and aligned with what your audience responds to, ultimately helping to increase the ROI of your email marketing efforts.

In navigating the intricacies of email marketing, from building a solid list to engaging with tailored content and optimizing through testing, you are equipping your business with a powerful tool to reach out directly to your customers and engage with them in meaningful ways. This direct line boosts your marketing efforts and enhances the overall customer experience, fostering loyalty and encouraging repeat business. As we move forward, remember that each email is not just a marketing message; it's a building block in the ongoing relationship between your brand and your customers.

6.4 GUERRILLA MARKETING TACTICS FOR MAXIMUM IMPACT

Understanding Guerrilla Marketing involves grasping the essence of making a significant marketing impact with minimal expenditure. This marketing style relies heavily on creativity, surprise elements, and unconventional strategies to grab the public's attention dramatically. For startups, guerrilla marketing can be a game-changer, allowing them to achieve visibility and memorability in a crowded market without the hefty advertising budgets that larger companies might command. The core idea is to utilize the environment around you to stage impactful marketing stunts that spark conversations and enhance brand recognition. For instance, imagine using sidewalk chalks to create intriguing art that leads to your store or projecting a captivating message onto a popular building downtown at night. These tactics draw attention due to their unexpected nature and create a buzz, encouraging people to share their experiences on social media and amplifying your marketing message without extensive resources.

Brainstorming and implementing creative guerrilla marketing campaigns on a tight budget requires thinking outside the box and an acute understanding of your audience's behaviors and preferences. You can start by identifying high-traffic areas that your target demographic frequently visits and think of ways to integrate your message into these spaces in an engaging and nonintrusive manner. For example, if your target audience includes young parents, consider setting up an impromptu play area with branded toys and games in a local park. Here, the key is subtlety—your brand's presence should feel natural within the setting rather than forced. Another effective tactic is to create an element of mystery around your campaign. This could be as simple as distributing parts of a puzzle throughout the city, which, when pieced together, reveal a special discount code or a message about your product. The intrigue alone will drive engagement, as people love solving mysteries, especially when a reward is at stake. Remember, the goal of guerrilla marketing is not just to be seen but to engage the community in an experience that feels personal and memorable.

Measuring the impact of your guerrilla marketing tactics is crucial to understanding their effectiveness and how they can be improved in future campaigns. Unlike traditional marketing methods, guerrilla marketing often relies on the campaign's virality, which can be somewhat challenging to measure. However, you can use several indicators to gauge the performance of your efforts. Social media engagement metrics such as likes, shares, comments, and mentions can provide insights into how much your campaign resonated with people. Tools like Google Analytics can help track any spikes in website traffic or increases in new users around the time of the campaign. Another method is to use specific hashtags associated with your guerrilla marketing stunt to monitor conversations and sentiments around your brand. Additionally, direct customer feedback through surveys or informal interactions can offer qualitative data that highlights the strengths and weaknesses of your campaign. Collecting and analyzing this data helps you measure your current campaign's success and refine your strategies for future marketing efforts.

Ethical Considerations in guerrilla marketing are paramount to ensure that while your campaigns are bold and attention-grabbing, they do not cross lines that could harm your brand's reputation. The first rule is to respect public space and private property. Any campaign involving public areas should be carefully planned to avoid disruption, damage, or inconvenience to the public. For instance, a flash mob in a city park should be organized to ensure it does not interfere with other events or the general public's enjoyment of the space. Furthermore, the content of your guerrilla marketing must be sensitive to cultural and social norms. Avoid tactics that could be perceived as offensive or insensitive, as the backlash could negate any positive impact your campaign might have had. Transparency is also critical; customers should not feel deceived or manipulated by your marketing tactics. Instead, they should be left with a positive impression of your brand as innovative and thoughtful. Keeping these ethical considerations in mind ensures that your guerrilla marketing efforts build your brand up rather than risk its integrity.

6.5 HARNESSING THE POWER OF CUSTOMER REVIEWS AND TESTIMONIALS

In the bustling marketplace of today, where choices abound, customer reviews and testimonials stand as potent markers of credibility and trustworthiness. Encouraging your satisfied customers to share their positive experiences is not merely about gathering accolades; it's about converting their satisfaction into a compelling narrative for potential customers. Initiating this process can be as simple as sending follow-up emails thanking customers for their purchase and kindly asking them to leave a review. Alternatively, integrating a review system directly on your product pages or third-party review platforms can streamline the process. Incentivizing reviews with small perks like discounts or entry into a giveaway can further motivate customers to share their thoughts. Notably, the key to genuine positive reviews is creating an exceptional product and customer experience that customers want to rave about naturally.

Once you have gathered these testimonials, leveraging them effectively comes into play. Promising or showcasing reviews on your website through social media can significantly influence buying behavior. Testimonials can be compelling when matched with specific products or services, providing real-life endorsements that resonate more deeply than any self-promotion. Crafting stories around these testimonials through a featured blog post or a video series of customer stories can amplify their impact. These narratives illustrate the value of your offerings and humanize your brand, fostering a deeper connection with your audience.

However, not all feedback will glow with positivity. Managing negative feedback constructively is crucial to maintaining your brand's reputation. First, responding promptly and professionally is essential, as well as acknowledging the customer's concerns and expressing your commitment to resolving the issue. Offering a solution or compensation where appropriate can often turn a dissatisfied customer into a loyal one. Importantly, each negative review provides a unique insight into possible areas of improvement for your product or service. Embracing this feedback as an opportunity for growth can significantly enhance your offerings, ultimately reducing the likelihood of future complaints.

Building trust through reviews and testimonials hinges on authenticity. Potential customers are increasingly savvy in recognizing genuine feedback from manufactured endorsements, so ensuring that real customers verify your reviews is essential. Transparency about your review process, such as noting that reviews are verified purchases, can also help build trust. Over time, a consistent accumulation of genuine, positive reviews will enhance your brand's credibility, making potential customers feel more secure in choosing your products or services.

In conclusion, customer reviews and testimonials are invaluable assets in your marketing arsenal. They prove your product's value and enhance your brand's reliability and customer loyalty. By actively encouraging reviews, effectively leveraging them in your marketing efforts, professionally handling negative feedback, and building trust through authenticity, you can significantly amplify your brand's reputation and desirability in the market. As we transition from exploring the dynamic world of direct customer engagement through reviews to understanding the broader implications of operational strategies in the next chapter, keep in mind that each customer interaction, whether highlighted in a review or not, shapes the narrative of your brand and its journey towards enduring success.

CHAPTER 7

OPERATIONS AND WORKFLOW OPTIMIZATION

Imagine stepping into a workspace that doesn't just welcome you but enhances your creativity and productivity from the moment you walk in. This isn't just about having a tidy desk or a good computer; it's about creating an environment that fundamentally transforms how you work, making every task smoother and every decision clearer. In this chapter, we dive deep into setting up your workspace for ultimate success, ensuring that every element, from the layout of your desk to the software you use, is optimized for efficiency and comfort. Whether you're working from a bustling office or the quiet corner of your home, the principles of effective workspace design can elevate your performance and mitigate the inevitable fatigue that comes from chasing your dreams.

7.1 SETTING UP YOUR WORKSPACE FOR SUCCESS

Ergonomic Design: Creating a workspace that boosts productivity and minimizes fatigue

Ergonomics isn't just a buzzword; it's a foundational element in designing a workspace that enhances your well-being and efficiency. Please start with the chair you sit in; it should support your back with adjustable features to fit your body perfectly, preventing strain during those long work hours. Your desk height and the position of your monitor should encourage a posture that keeps your back straight and your eyes level with the top of the screen, reducing neck strain. Consider the lighting as well—natural light is ideal, but if that's not possible, ensure your artificial lighting is bright enough to prevent eye strain yet soft enough to avoid harsh glares on your screen. These adjustments might seem minor, but they significantly boost your productivity and protect your health.

Efficient Layout: Organizing your physical and digital workspace for maximum efficiency

An efficient layout extends beyond physical space into the digital realm. Physically, keep frequently used tools within arm's reach and maintain a clutter-free desk, which can help reduce cognitive overload and keep you focused. Digitally organize your computer desktop and files in a clear, logical system, so you're not spending unnecessary time searching for documents or tools. Use desktop organizers or drawer dividers to keep your physical workspace orderly. Employ file management software or cloud services to categorize and quickly retrieve files for your digital space neatly.

This dual approach to organizing your physical and digital spaces can dramatically reduce wasted time and streamline your workflow, making your day-to-day operations smoother and more intuitive.

Distraction-Free Environment: Strategies to minimize distractions and maintain focus

In today's world, distractions are just a click away. Creating a distraction-free environment starts with identifying what distracts you the most—social media, emails, or noisy office environments. Tools like website blockers can help limit your access to distracting sites during work hours, helping you stay focused on the tasks. If noise is a distraction, noise-canceling headphones can be invaluable, whether playing calming music or enjoying the silence. Additionally, setting specific times to check emails or messages rather than responding to notifications immediately can help maintain your focus and drastically improve your productivity. Cultivate a practice of deep work by scheduling uninterrupted blocks of time where you focus solely on one task. This method increases the quality of your work and speeds up completion times, allowing you to accomplish more with less stress.

Tools for Remote Work: Essential tools and practices for managing a remote or hybrid team effectively

The rise of remote and hybrid work models has introduced new challenges in maintaining operational efficiency and team cohesion. Comprehensive communication and project management tools are vital to managing a remote team effectively. Platforms like Slack for communication and Asana for project management keep everyone on the same page, regardless of their physical location. Regular video meetings can also help maintain a sense of team unity and ensure alignment on projects. Beyond tools, establish clear expectations and regular check-ins to monitor progress and address any issues promptly. Foster a culture of openness where team members feel comfortable sharing their challenges. These practices help streamline project workflows and support a healthy, engaged, productive remote team.

By carefully designing your workspace and employing strategic tools and practices, you can create an environment that maximizes productivity and supports your physical and mental health, making your entrepreneurial path smoother and more enjoyable. As we continue to explore the complexities of operational efficiency, these foundational aspects of workspace optimization will act as the building blocks for more advanced strategies, ensuring that you are well-equipped to handle the challenges of growing your business. Remember, a well-organized and thoughtfully designed workspace is not a luxury—it's a crucial element in cultivating a successful and sustainable business operation.

7.2 TOOLS AND TECHNOLOGIES TO BOOST YOUR PRODUCTIVITY

In the fast-paced world where every second counts, especially for entrepreneurs striving to carve out their niche, the judicious selection and application of technology can be your greatest ally. Choosing the right software tools is about filling up your digital toolbox and strategically selecting those that seamlessly integrate into and enhance your business operations. Think of software as your silent partner that works diligently behind the scenes—its primary role is to streamline workflows, reduce errors, and free up your time to focus on core business activities. For instance, robust accounting software manages your books and provides insightful financial reporting that aids strategic decision-making. Similarly, customer relationship management (CRM) systems can automate and fine-tune your customer interactions, ensuring you maintain strong relationships without dropping the ball. When selecting software, consider scalability, user-friendliness, and integration capabilities with your existing tools. It's also wise to opt for software that offers robust customer support and ensures help is available whenever needed.

The potential of automation in the modern business landscape cannot be overstated. By implementing automation tools, you can delegate routine and repetitive tasks to technology, allowing you to focus on areas that require human creativity and decision-making. From scheduling social media posts to managing email campaigns and processing orders, automation can take over many mundane tasks. Moreover, automation extends to data entry and analysis, where tools equipped with artificial intelligence can perform complex data analysis, providing you with insights that would take days to compile manually. The key to effective automation is identifying repetitive and time-consuming processes without requiring human oversight. Start small by automating single tasks, and as you become comfortable, gradually expand to more complex processes. This approach improves efficiency and reduces the likelihood of human error, ensuring smoother operations.

Leveraging collaboration platforms is crucial as businesses increasingly embrace remote and hybrid work models. These platforms enhance communication and teamwork by providing a shared space where team members can collaborate on projects in real time, regardless of their physical location. Tools like Microsoft Teams or Slack facilitate instant messaging and file sharing, while platforms like Trello or Monday. com offer visual project management features that help track tasks and deadlines. The real magic of these platforms lies in their ability to keep everyone aligned on their goals and progress, fostering a collaborative spirit and making teamwork more effective. When choosing a collaboration platform, consider your team's specific needs, including the size of your team, the nature of your projects, and the complexity required in project management. Additionally, look for usability features like mobile access, integration with other tools, and customizable notifications.

Data security in today's digital-first environment is paramount. As you integrate more digital tools into your business operations, the risk of data breaches and cyber threats looms larger. Protecting sensitive information—financial data, customer information, or proprietary business insights—is crucial for your business's reputation and compliance with data protection regulations. Start by ensuring your software and tools comply with industry-standard data security protocols. Invest in robust antivirus software and firewalls, and establish secure backup systems to protect your data from loss due to system failures or cyber-attacks. Educating your team on basic data security practices, such as recognizing phishing attempts and using strong, unique passwords, is also vital. For businesses handling particularly sensitive data, consider consulting with cybersecurity experts to implement advanced security strategies tailored to your needs.

Selecting and utilizing the right tools and technologies can significantly enhance operational efficiency and security. These technologies support your current business operations and scale with your growth, ensuring that your systems can handle increased demands without compromising performance or security as your business evolves.

7.3 CREATING SYSTEMS AND PROCESSES FOR SCALABILITY

Imagine your business as a living organism that grows and evolves. Just as a tree strengthens its roots to support a broader canopy, your business needs robust systems and processes that can adapt and scale as your operations expand. Developing Standard Operating Procedures (SOPs) is like laying down a network of roots, providing the foundational support that ensures every part of your business functions effectively and consistently, regardless of size or complexity. SOPs are detailed, written instructions describing how to carry out a routine activity within your company. They are crucial for maintaining quality and efficiency, especially as your team grows. For instance, an SOP for handling customer inquiries might detail everything from the tone of voice to be used to the steps for logging the investigation in a tracking system. These procedures ensure that all team members, whether veterans or new hires, handle tasks that align with your business's standards and objectives uniformly.

As your business develops, anticipating and planning for future needs becomes essential. Scalability planning involves looking at where your business will be in the next five, ten, or even twenty years and mapping out the systems supporting this growth. This might mean investing in scalable cloud-based technology platforms that can handle increasing data loads or designing flexible business processes that can be easily adjusted as you enter new markets or expand your product lines. It's about thinking big picture— ensuring that your decisions today won't limit your options tomorrow. For example, suppose you anticipate your customer base doubling within the following year. In that case, you might implement a customer relationship management (CRM) system that meets your current needs and can quickly scale to handle increased demand.

Delegation is a critical skill that you must hone as your business grows. Creating clear frameworks for delegation ensures that responsibilities are not just handed off but are done so in a way that everyone involved understands their tasks and the standards to which they are held. Effective delegation isn't about relinquishing control but empowering your team by entrusting them with responsibilities aligning with their strengths and skills. This involves clear communication, setting expectations, and providing the necessary resources. For instance, when you delegate the task of report preparation, please specify the report's required elements, the data sources, the format, and the deadline. Provide templates and examples, and be available to answer questions. By systematizing delegation, you ensure that tasks are completed efficiently and correctly, freeing up your time to focus on strategic growth activities.

Establishing feedback mechanisms is another cornerstone of scalable systems. These mechanisms should be designed to continually collect and analyze data on the effectiveness of your processes and the satisfaction of your clients and employees. This could be as simple as regular feedback surveys or more integrated systems like quality checks embedded into your production lines. The key is to create a loop where feedback leads to actions that improve your systems and processes, which should be re-evaluated for effectiveness. For example, after implementing a new order fulfillment process, you might track the average time to fill orders and the error rate and then gather team feedback to identify any issues or bottlenecks. This ongoing feedback cycle and improvement helps your business stay aligned with best practices and customer expectations, even as it grows and changes.

By embedding these scalable systems and processes into the fabric of your business, you lay the groundwork for sustainable growth and success. Each element—from SOPs and scalability planning to delegation frameworks and feedback loops—is crucial in ensuring your business can adapt and thrive in an ever-changing marketplace. As you continue to build and refine these systems, remember that the true strength of your business lies not just in its products or services but in the robustness of its operations and the agility with which it can respond to new challenges and opportunities.

7.4 HIRING YOUR FIRST EMPLOYEES: WHEN AND HOW TO EXPAND YOUR TEAM

Understanding when and who to hire can often feel like trying to solve a complex puzzle where each piece must fit perfectly to complete the picture of your growing business. The decision to expand your team should be driven by clear business growth indicators and an assessment of your current team's capacity to meet demand. Start by evaluating the workload and the impact on service delivery or product quality. Do you know if deadlines are being missed? Is customer service suffering? These signs point to the need for additional hands. It's also crucial to consider future projects or expansions and the skills required to execute them effectively. Hiring with foresight involves not just filling immediate gaps but anticipating the skills and roles you will need down the line. For example, hiring a digital marketing expert now could be a strategic move if you expand your digital presence.

Once you've identified the need to hire, crafting a recruitment strategy that attracts the right talent is your next step. This begins with a clear and compelling job description that outlines the role and responsibilities and highlights what makes your startup a unique workplace. Please emphasize growth opportunities, your company's mission and values, and any unique benefits you offer. Utilizing the proper recruitment channels is equally important. While job boards are an everyday go-to, consider industry-specific forums, social media platforms, and professional networking sites like LinkedIn, which can help you tap into a wider pool of potential candidates. Moreover, leveraging your existing networks or employee referrals can often lead to finding candidates who are an excellent cultural fit with your organization. It is essential to make a selection process that looks at the candidates' technical abilities and experience and their alignment with your company's culture and values. Techniques such as behavioral interviews, practical assignments, or trial periods can provide deeper insight into a candidate's suitability.

Integrating new employees into your team effectively begins with a structured onboarding process. This is your opportunity to set them up for success from day one. Effective onboarding goes beyond just reviewing job duties and office policies; it should immerse new hires in your company culture and connect them with their colleagues immediately. Start with a welcome session that helps them build a comprehensive understanding of your business, its goals, and its role in achieving these goals. Assign a mentor or buddy from your existing team to guide them through their first few weeks. This helps with the practical aspects of their job and integrates them into the team socially. Regular check-ins during the first few months can also help address any questions or concerns as they settle into their role. Remember, a well-thought-out onboarding process can significantly impact employee satisfaction, retention, and productivity.

Cultivating a positive company culture is pivotal as it shapes the employee experience and defines your brand identity internally. A strong culture is built on clear values practiced at every level of the organization, not just on your website. Encourage open communication, foster a team-oriented environment, and recognize and reward contributions and achievements. Activities that build camaraderie, such as team outings or lunch-and-learns, can strengthen relationships among team members. Also, please make sure you actively seek and act upon feedback from your team. This can involve regular one-on-one meetings, anonymous surveys, or suggestion boxes. Such practices help maintain a pulse on the team's morale and foster a culture of continuous improvement. Remember, a culture that supports and values employees not only aids in retention but also attracts top talent, setting a solid foundation for your business's continued growth and success.

By methodically addressing these critical areas in your hiring process, you ensure that each new team member fits the role and is a valuable addition to your company culture, contributing to your business's vision and long-term objectives.

7.5 OUTSOURCING FOR EFFICIENCY: WHAT TASKS TO DELEGATE

As your business grows, so does the complexity of the tasks it must manage daily. There comes a point when doing everything in-house might not be the most efficient or cost-effective strategy. That's where outsourcing steps in as a strategic tool, allowing you to delegate specific tasks to external professionals who can perform them more efficiently or at a lower cost. Identifying which tasks to outsource is crucial and should focus on non-core but time-consuming tasks or require specialized skills that your team might not possess. For instance, if digital marketing isn't your forte, outsourcing it to a specialized agency can free up your time and potentially bring better results. Similarly, successful businesses often outsource tasks like payroll processing, customer support, and product development to harness specialized efficiencies and reduce workload.

Choosing the right outsourcing partners is as critical as deciding what to outsource. You can start by clearly defining what you need from an outsourcing partner, including the scope of work, expected outcomes, and the quality standards you expect. With these criteria, you can evaluate potential providers based on their expertise, reputation, and alignment with your business's values and goals. Requesting case studies or references from potential partners is advisable to understand better their capabilities and the results they've achieved for other clients. Additionally, consider the communication styles and tools they use. Effective communication is critical to managing outsourced tasks successfully, and you'll want a responsive and transparent partner.

Managing relationships with outsourcing providers is another critical component. Establish clear communication channels and regular check-ins to ensure alignment and address any issues as they arise. Setting up detailed contracts outlining each party's responsibilities, deliverables, timelines, and protocols for handling conflicts is also beneficial. Quality control should be a continuous part of the process. Regular reviews and audits of the work done ensure that the output meets your standards and expectations. Moreover, be prepared to invest time in training your providers about your business's processes and quality standards to ensure they fully understand your needs and expectations.

Performing a cost-benefit analysis is essential before and during outsourcing engagements. Evaluate the direct costs associated with hiring an external provider and the potential savings in time and resources. Also, consider the opportunity costs; what could your team achieve if freed from the tasks you plan to outsource? This analysis should also factor in the potential for scaling operations more quickly and the benefits of accessing specialized skills and technology. However, be mindful of the risks, including reduced control over certain aspects of your business and the potential for miscommunication or cultural misalignment, which can impact the quality of work.

Outsourcing can be a powerful strategy for streamlining operations, reducing costs, and enhancing flexibility and expertise within your business. By carefully selecting tasks to outsource, choosing the right partners, managing these relationships effectively, and continuously analyzing the costs and benefits, you can ensure that outsourcing contributes positively to your business growth and operational efficiency.

As we conclude this chapter on optimizing your operations and workflows, remember that the goal is to build a foundation that supports your current operations and scales seamlessly with your business's growth. The strategies discussed—from setting up an effective workspace to leveraging outsourcing—enhance operational efficiency and free up your internal resources to focus on core business activities. In the next chapter, we will explore financial management strategies that ensure your business remains profitable and financially healthy as it grows. This next step is crucial, as robust financial management forms the backbone of a sustainable business, enabling you to make informed decisions and secure your business's future in a competitive market.

CHAPTER 8

FINANCIAL MANAGEMENT FOR SUSTAINABLE GROWTH

Imagine steering a ship through the vast ocean, where every navigational choice directly impacts your journey to new horizons. Similarly, financial management is your compass and rudder in business, guiding your venture through economic currents and winds, ensuring you survive and thrive in the competitive marketplace. In this chapter, we delve into the foundational aspect of financial management—bookkeeping—a skill as crucial as the captain's ability to read the stars, ensuring that your business remains on course and your financial health is transparent and robust.

8.1 BOOKKEEPING BASICS FOR ENTREPRENEURS

Setting Up Your System: Choosing the right bookkeeping system that fits your business size and needs.

Choosing the right bookkeeping system is akin to selecting the right type of sail for your ship that will efficiently catch the wind and propel you forward. The size of your business, the complexity of your transactions, and the growth you anticipate all play critical roles in determining the ideal system. For small businesses, a simple spreadsheet might suffice initially, but as your business grows, investing in a more robust system like QuickBooks or Xero, which can automate much of the process, might become necessary. The key is to choose a system scalable enough to grow with your business and flexible enough to meet your changing needs. A system that can integrate with other tools, such as your point of sale (POS) system, payroll, and bank accounts, will streamline your processes and provide real-time financial data, which is invaluable for making informed business decisions.

Recording Transactions: Best practices for accurately recording financial transactions.

Accurate record-keeping is the cornerstone of sound financial management. No matter how small, each transaction should be recorded meticulously to ensure your financial statements are correct. This includes sales and expenses and less frequent transactions such as refunds, returns, and exchanges. Consistency is key—develop a daily, weekly, or monthly routine for how and when transactions are recorded. Use clear categories for income and expenses to simplify tracking and reporting. It's also wise to keep detailed notes explaining each transaction, which can be invaluable during tax season or if you are audited. Remember, accurate record-keeping aims to satisfy regulatory requirements and provide you with a clear snapshot of your financial health at any given moment, enabling proactive business management.

Financial Statements: Understanding and preparing basic financial statements (balance sheet, income statement).

Financial statements are your business's health reports. The balance sheet provides a snapshot of your business's financial position at a specific moment, showing what you own (assets) and owe (liabilities), with the difference being your equity. The income statement, or profit and loss statement, shows how much money you made and spent over a period, clearly showing your operational efficiency. Regularly preparing and reviewing these statements can help you understand where your money is coming from and where it is going, identify trends, and make informed strategic decisions. For entrepreneurs without a financial background, it might seem daunting. Still, many bookkeeping software options have features that automate much of this process, making it accessible regardless of your financial expertise.

Bookkeeping Software: Recommendations for software that can simplify the bookkeeping process.

In today's digital age, leveraging technology can significantly simplify bookkeeping. Software solutions like QuickBooks, Xero, and FreshBooks are designed with the user in mind, offering intuitive interfaces, automation of standard bookkeeping tasks, and easy integration with other business systems. These tools can handle everything from invoicing and payroll to reporting and tax preparation, providing comprehensive functionality that can save you time and reduce errors. When selecting bookkeeping software, consider cost, usability, customer support, and the specific features that align with your business needs. Many providers offer free trials, which can be a valuable opportunity to test whether the software meets your expectations before committing financially.

Interactive Element: Financial Health Checklist

To actively engage with your financial management processes, here's a practical checklist to ensure your bookkeeping is on track:

Daily Tasks:

- Record all financial transactions.
- Verify and categorize expenses.

Weekly Tasks:

- Review weekly financial summaries.
- Check cash flow statements for any discrepancies.

Monthly Tasks:

- Reconcile bank statements with your bookkeeping records.
- Prepare financial statements (balance sheet, income statement).
- Review monthly financial performance and adjust budgets as necessary.

Quarterly Tasks:

- Review quarterly tax obligations.
- Evaluate financial goals and progress towards them.

Annual Tasks:

- Prepare year-end financial reports.
- Assess annual performance and plan for the next fiscal year.

Utilizing this checklist can help maintain a rigorous financial discipline, ensuring your venture remains financially healthy and geared toward sustained growth. As you integrate these practices into your daily business operations, remember that each step in accurate bookkeeping and financial management secures your current position and steers you toward future prosperity and success.

8.2 CASH FLOW MANAGEMENT TECHNIQUES

Understanding the dynamics of cash flow is crucial for any business owner. Unlike profit, a theoretical figure reflecting earnings minus expenses over a specific period, cash flow represents the amount of money flowing in and out of your business at any given time. A company can be profitable on paper but still needs financial assistance if cash flow can be better managed. This is because cash flow impacts your ability to pay bills, purchase inventory, and invest in new opportunities at the right times. Imagine a scenario where your business secures a large order that significantly boosts your profits. However, suppose the payment terms for this order mean you won't receive the funds for 90 days. In that case, you might struggle to meet immediate financial obligations such as paying suppliers or covering payroll. This disconnect between profits and cash flow is a common pitfall that can threaten the stability and growth of your business.

Forecasting cash flow is a strategic exercise that involves predicting future financial inflows and outflows to ensure you have enough cash to cover your obligations and avoid financial strain. Effective cash flow forecasting requires understanding your financial situation and potential future scenarios. Tools such as spreadsheets can be powerful for modeling your cash flow, allowing you to input various assumptions based on past business performance and future projections. For instance, you can model expected sales increases due to a new marketing campaign or predict slower cash inflows during off-peak seasons. More sophisticated tools like cash flow management software offer real-time data integration and predictive analytics, providing a more dynamic and accurate forecast. Regularly updating your estimates as you gain more data and insight into business trends and market conditions will help you stay one step ahead, ensuring you're never caught off guard by cash flow fluctuations.

Improving cash flow is often about timing and efficiency. One effective strategy is accelerating the inflows while delaying the outflows without compromising your relationships with suppliers or customers. For example, you might offer discounts to customers who pay their invoices early. This can encourage faster payments, boosting your cash flow when needed. On the outflow side, negotiate longer payment terms with suppliers to keep the cash within your business longer before it is paid out. However, it's crucial to maintain a good rapport with your suppliers to ensure you don't jeopardize critical business relationships. Additionally, regularly reviewing your expenses and cutting down on non-essential spending can free up cash, making it available for areas of your business that generate direct returns on investment. Automating invoice and payment systems can also reduce delays and the labor costs associated with manual processing, further improving your cash flow.

Dealing with cash crunches requires a proactive and strategic approach. The key is to identify potential cash flow problems before they occur and have a plan to address them. One approach is establishing a line of credit with a bank before you need it. This can provide a financial buffer to draw on when cash flow is tighter than expected. I would also like to ensure you have multiple financing options available. During a cash crunch, prioritize your payments, focusing on critical business operations, such as essential supplier payments that keep your product or service deliverable. Communication is also vital; if you foresee a delay in payment, it's better to communicate with creditors to negotiate more favorable terms rather than missing payments without notice. Additionally, keeping an eye on your cash conversion cycle can help you identify how quickly the resources invested in your business are turning into cash flows from sales. If this cycle is too slow, strategies such as reducing inventory levels or speeding up production processes might be necessary.

Managing cash flow effectively is not just about keeping your business afloat; it's about setting a stable foundation for growth and flexibility, allowing you to seize opportunities and confidently navigate challenges. As you continue to explore the financial aspects of your business, remember that cash flow is a critical indicator of your business's health and operational efficiency, reflecting not just your financial planning skills but also your ability to adapt to the ever-changing dynamics of business economics.

8.3 UNDERSTANDING AND MAXIMIZING PROFIT MARGINS

Profit margins are more than just numbers on a financial statement; they are vital indicators of your business's health and efficiency. Understanding how to calculate and interpret these figures is akin to a doctor reading vital signs to assess a patient's health. Essentially, profit margin measures how much out of every dollar of sales a company keeps in earnings, which is crucial for determining the profitability of your business. To calculate your profit margin, you would subtract total expenses from total revenue to find the net profit, divide that net profit by the total income, and multiply by 100 to get a percentage. This percentage tells you how many cents of profit your business has generated for each dollar of sale. For instance, a 20% profit margin means you keep $0.20 from each dollar of sales revenue. This metric is invaluable as it provides insights into various aspects of your business operations, from pricing strategy to cost management, and helps you gauge your business's financial health compared to competitors in your industry.

Cost reduction strategies are essential for improving your profit margins. It's about making smarter spending decisions without compromising the quality of your products or services. Start by analyzing your current expenses to identify areas where costs can be cut or optimized. For example, if you're manufacturing a product, look at the cost of materials and explore if bulk purchasing or negotiating with suppliers could reduce costs. In the same way, if you're running a service-based business, please review your operational expenses. Could you reduce office space costs by implementing a hybrid work model or cut utility expenses by investing in energy-efficient equipment? Reducing overhead can directly increase your profit margins by lowering the costs of producing your goods or services. Additionally, automating repetitive tasks should be considered to reduce labor costs. Automation software can manage functions like scheduling, invoicing, and customer communications, which cuts costs and allows your team to focus on more strategic activities that could drive revenue.

Pricing strategies also play a pivotal role in maximizing profitability while staying competitive. Setting the right price for your products or services involves understanding your market, customers, and competitors. One effective strategy is value-based pricing, which consists of setting prices primarily on the perceived value to the customer rather than on the cost of the product or historical prices. This approach can be convenient if your business offers unique features that stand out from competitors. Another strategy is psychological pricing, which uses pricing techniques to influence perception, such as pricing a product at $99 instead of $100. The idea is to make the price appear lower than it is to boost sales, which can, in turn, increase your profit margins. It's crucial, however, to continuously monitor the market and adjust your pricing strategies accordingly to respond to new competitors or changes in customer demand to ensure your pricing strategy remains effective.

Monitoring your profit margins is not a set-it-and-forget-it task; it requires ongoing attention and adjustment. This involves regularly reviewing your financial statements to track whether your profit margins are improving or deteriorating. It's also wise to monitor industry trends and benchmark against them. Are your margins better or worse than the industry average? It might signal that you need to cut costs or change your pricing strategy if they're worse. If they're better, it's a validation of your current methods, but it doesn't mean there's no room for improvement.

Regularly revisiting your cost reduction strategies and pricing model can help you find new ways to enhance your profitability. Implementing a dashboard that provides a real-time view of your financial metrics can also help you monitor these figures more effectively, allowing for quicker adjustments in strategies to protect your profit margins in a dynamic market environment.

Navigating the complexities of profit margins involves balancing cost efficiency, setting strategic prices, and constantly monitoring financial health. This proactive management of profit margins ensures your business survives and thrives, regardless of market conditions, maintaining a competitive edge and achieving sustainable growth.

8.4 NAVIGATING TAXES FOR NEW BUSINESS OWNERS

Navigating the realm of taxes is akin to decoding a complex map where each turn and symbol has significant implications for your business journey. I'd like to point out that understanding the tax obligations that apply specifically to your business structure and industry is the first critical step. Different business structures, sole proprietorships, partnerships, LLCs, or corporations come with distinct tax responsibilities. For instance, while sole proprietors report business income and expenses via their personal tax returns, corporations may be subject to double taxation—once at the corporate level and again on dividends paid to shareholders. Additionally, your industry might dictate specific tax considerations, such as excise taxes for products like alcohol or tobacco. Familiarizing yourself with these nuances ensures compliance and helps identify potential tax advantages that could be leveraged.

Tax planning is an ongoing process that involves strategizing how to conduct business affairs in ways that minimize or defer tax liabilities without breaching legal boundaries. Effective tax planning entails making astute decisions throughout the year, not just at the year-end, about when to incur expenses and how to structure transactions. It can also involve selecting the correct type of business entity that offers optimal tax benefits for your situation and planning for large expenditures in ways that maximize tax breaks—for instance, timing the purchase of significant equipment to coincide with tax periods where it can yield greater deductions. Strategic use of retirement plans can also serve dual purposes—securing your financial future while reducing taxable income. The aim is to create a plan that reduces your overall tax burden while enhancing your business's economic outcomes.

Keeping meticulous records is not merely a practice of good governance but a critical necessity for tax purposes. Efficient record-keeping ensures that every transaction can be substantiated, which is crucial during tax audits. It involves more than just retaining receipts—it means maintaining comprehensive records of incomes, expenses, deductions, and credits. The method of accounting you choose, whether cash or accrual, also affects how transactions are recorded. For example, income is recorded when received using the cash method, and expenses are paid. This method could be beneficial for managing tax outflows based on actual cash flow rather than anticipated earnings or costs. Proper documentation supports filing accurate tax returns and validating claims for deductions, exemptions, and credits, which can significantly lower tax liabilities.

Seeking professional help from a tax advisor or accountant isn't just for those moments when you feel overwhelmed; it's a proactive approach to ensure your business complies with tax laws and benefits from potential tax-saving opportunities. Tax professionals stay abreast of the latest changes in tax legislation that could affect your business. They can provide invaluable guidance on complex tax issues, help in strategic tax planning, and represent you in dealings with tax authorities. Especially for new business owners, investing in professional tax advice can prevent costly mistakes and penalties associated with non-compliance. It can also free up your time and energy to focus on growing your business and ensure your tax affairs are in order.

As we wrap up this exploration into the essential realm of financial management for your business, from bookkeeping fundamentals to sophisticated tax strategies, remember that each component plays a crucial role in shaping your business's economic health. These practices ensure compliance and optimization of financial resources and build a robust framework that supports your business's growth and scalability.

Up next, we venture into strategies for growth and expansion, exploring how to leverage your solid financial foundation to scale new heights in the competitive business landscape. Here, the financial acumen you've cultivated will be instrumental in navigating the challenges and seizing the opportunities of expanding your business.

CHAPTER 9

STRATEGIES FOR GROWTH AND EXPANSION

Imagine your business is a thriving garden. You've nurtured the soil, planted the seeds, and watched with pride as the sprouts have grown into vigorous, healthy plants. Now, you're contemplating whether it's the right time to expand your garden, introduce new varieties of plants, or perhaps extend the boundaries further than ever before. This chapter is about recognizing when your business, like a well-tended garden, is ready to flourish and expand beyond its current confines. It's about understanding the signs of readiness, preparing for the scalability of operations, and strategically planning to ensure that the growth is sustainable and doesn't outpace your capacity to manage effectively. Let's explore how to scale your business with precision and foresight.

9.1 WHEN AND HOW TO SCALE YOUR BUSINESS

Assessing Scalability: Determining if your business model is ready for scaling.

Scaling your business is exhilarating, but assessing whether your current business model can handle growth is vital. This means examining the core components of your operations, from your supply chain logistics to customer service protocols, to ensure they can be expanded without sacrificing quality or efficiency. Questions to consider include: Can your supply chain manage increased orders? Do you know if you have the technology in place to support more customers or clients? Is your team equipped to handle a more significant workload? Answering these questions will help you gauge whether your business model is robust enough for scaling or if tweaks are needed to prepare for growth.

Growth Indicators: Identifying key indicators that signal it's time to scale.

Recognizing the right time to scale is crucial and can be indicated by several key factors. Consistent increase in demand for your products or services, reaching or exceeding sales targets over multiple quarters, and increased market opportunities are clear indicators that scaling could be the next step. Additionally, if your business has strong operational cash flow and a solid customer base, these are signs that your business is on stable ground, which is crucial for supporting expansion. Monitoring these indicators can give you confidence that scaling is not just a possibility but a prudent decision.

Scaling Plan: Developing a comprehensive plan for scaling operations, teams, and infrastructure.

Once you've decided to scale, the next step is to develop a strategic scaling plan. This involves detailed planning across several aspects of your business. Operationally, consider what needs to be upgraded or expanded: production facilities, office space, or IT infrastructure. From a team perspective, identify the roles that will be crucial for supporting growth and begin the recruitment process accordingly. Enhancing your team's skills and capabilities through training programs is also wise. Infrastructure-wise, assess whether your current systems, such as CRM and ERP systems, can handle increased loads or need to be replaced or upgraded. Documenting every step in your scaling plan gives you a clear roadmap. It helps communicate this growth strategy to your team and stakeholders, ensuring everyone is aligned and committed to the vision.

Avoiding Overexpansion: Strategies to avoid the pitfalls of scaling too quickly.

Scaling too quickly can be as detrimental as not scaling at all. It's critical to pace your growth to avoid the pitfalls of overexpansion. Ensure that every step of your scaling plan is sustainable—from financial expenditures to hiring. Implementing rigorous financial checks and balances, setting realistic growth targets, and maintaining a capital reserve can safeguard against overextension. Additionally, cultivate a flexible business culture that can adapt to changes and challenges that come with scaling. Being prepared to recalibrate your growth strategy in response to market feedback or operational difficulties is crucial. This adaptability can be the difference between successful scaling and overexpansion, which could lead your business into operational and financial problems.

Scaling your business is a significant step that comes with challenges and opportunities. By carefully assessing your readiness, recognizing the right time to grow, planning strategically, and being cautious of overexpansion, you can ensure that this next phase of your business lifecycle is successful and sustainable. Embrace this growth with the same care and strategic planning that you would tend to a growing garden, and watch as your business reaches new heights of success.

9.2 EXPLORING NEW MARKETS AND VERTICALS

When you're ready to take your business beyond its current boundaries, exploring new markets and verticals can be a thrilling next step. But this move requires thorough preparation and understanding of the new terrain. You'll need to conduct detailed market research. It would be best to dig deep into potential markets to uncover the demographic and economic conditions, the competitive landscape, and consumer behaviors. Tools such as market analysis reports, consumer surveys, and data analytics platforms can provide invaluable insights. For instance, data analytics to track online consumer behavior and preferences in a specific geographic region can help you understand what potential customers might expect from your product or service. Additionally, attending industry conferences and networking with local businesses can provide a nuanced market understanding that broad data can only sometimes offer.

Once you've identified a promising new market, adapting your product or service to fit this new context is essential. This might mean tweaking your product design, altering your service offerings, or overhauling your branding to resonate with local tastes and cultural norms. For example, if expanding into a market where environmental sustainability is highly valued, consider adapting your product to meet eco-friendly standards, which could involve changing your production processes or materials to align with local environmental regulations and consumer expectations. Tailoring your marketing messages to address local issues and incorporating regional languages or dialects in your advertising and customer service can also significantly enhance your market entry strategy.

Practical tactics for entering and establishing a presence in new markets vary widely but often include a mix of strategic partnerships, localized marketing campaigns, and sometimes even establishing a physical presence in the market through offices or distribution centers. A gradual, phased approach can be particularly practical, starting with a limited rollout to test the waters, followed by a full launch if the initial phase meets or exceeds your benchmarks. For instance, launching a pilot program that introduces your product to a small market segment allows you to gather real-time feedback and adjust your approach before a full-scale launch. Digital platforms can also play a crucial role in these strategies, enabling you to create targeted, localized marketing campaigns that can be adjusted quickly based on market response.

Cultural considerations are paramount when entering new markets. Every market has unique cultural nuances that can dramatically influence consumer behavior. Understanding these subtleties can distinguish between resonating with your new audience or missing the mark entirely. This involves more than just translating your marketing materials into another language. It requires understanding cultural symbols, communication styles, and purchasing behaviors. For instance, color symbolism varies significantly between cultures; a color representing prosperity in one culture may have negative connotations in another. Similarly, negotiation practices and business meeting etiquette can differ, and what is considered persuasive in one culture might be seen as aggressive or off-putting in another. Engaging local experts or cultural consultants can provide deep insights into these aspects, helping you navigate the complex cultural landscapes of new markets effectively.

You can successfully navigate and establish a strong presence in new markets and verticals by meticulously researching, strategically adapting your offerings, employing thoughtful entry tactics, and profoundly understanding cultural nuances. This strategic expansion diversifies your business operations and opens new revenue streams, propelling your business toward more tremendous success and influence in the global marketplace.

9.3 PRODUCT DIVERSIFICATION: EXPANDING YOUR OFFERINGS

Diversifying your product line is akin to planting various seeds in your garden, each capable of flourishing under different conditions, thus ensuring stability and continued growth regardless of external changes. The benefits of diversification are manifold; primarily, it spreads risk across a broader range, safeguarding your business against the failure of a single product or market downturn. Moreover, introducing new products can tap into unexplored customer segments, potentially increasing market share and revenue streams. For instance, a company specializing in gourmet coffee might consider diversifying into coffee accessories or offering specialized tea blends, attracting tea drinkers and providing existing customers with new products to enhance their coffee experience.

Identifying new product or service opportunities requires understanding market trends, customer feedback, and competitive analysis. One effective method is to conduct customer satisfaction surveys that include questions about potential products, which can gauge interest and gather direct feedback. Additionally, keeping an eye on industry trends through trade publications and market reports can highlight new opportunities. For example, the rise in consumer interest in sustainability could lead an electronics manufacturer to explore product lines emphasizing energy efficiency and eco-friendly materials. Another method is to analyze your sales data for patterns that suggest complementary products. If customers often buy two products together, they can combine them into a new offering that better meets their needs.

The product development process for new offerings involves several key stages, beginning with idea generation. This initial phase should encourage creativity and be open to suggestions from all areas of your business, including marketing, customer service, and even supply chain operations. Once a viable idea is identified, it moves into the concept development stage, where feasibility studies are conducted. This stage answers critical questions about the product's design, production costs, market potential, and profitability. Following this, the product undergoes detailed design and development, during which prototypes are created and pilot runs are conducted to ensure the product meets design specifications and quality standards. After successful testing and refinement, the product is finally ready for launch.

Integrating new products into existing market efforts requires strategic planning to ensure they complement rather than cannibalize your current offerings. This integration can be facilitated through bundling, where new products are offered as part of a package deal with existing products, providing a seamless introduction to the market and adding value to the customer. Marketing plays a crucial role here, with targeted campaigns designed to highlight the benefits of the new product while reinforcing the brand's core values. For instance, if a fitness apparel company known for its durable products introduces a new line of eco-friendly workout gear, it should emphasize the environmental benefits and how the new line maintains the durability and performance standards customers expect. Social media platforms, email marketing, and in-store promotions effectively raise awareness and drive interest in new product offerings.

Expanding your product offerings through diversification is a strategic approach that can increase your business's resilience and profitability.

By carefully selecting opportunities, meticulously planning product development, and strategically integrating new products into the market, you can ensure that this expansion contributes positively to your business's growth and enhances your competitive edge in the marketplace.

9.4 BUILDING AND MANAGING A TEAM FOR GROWTH

Building a team that not only meets the current needs of your business but is also primed for future growth is akin to preparing a ship for a voyage across growing seas. The structure of your team and its ability to scale as your business expands are crucial. Designing a team structure to support growth involves creating scalable and adaptable roles, ensuring they can evolve as business needs become more complex. Consider implementing a modular structure where teams are built around critical functions but can easily be adjusted or expanded. This flexibility allows you to add or redefine new roles as your company grows, ensuring that vital functions are always adequately supported. For instance, you are starting with a core marketing team that can expand by adding specialists in areas like digital marketing or customer analytics as your market reach grows. This approach makes scaling smoother and helps manage resources more effectively, ensuring you can ramp up or scale down quickly based on business performance and market conditions.

Recruiting strategies to attract talent that aligns with your growth goals are next. In today's competitive job market, attracting the right talent involves more than offering a good salary. It's about portraying your company as a place where ambitious professionals can thrive and make a significant impact. Start by crafting job descriptions that communicate not just the roles but the potential for growth and the impact these roles have on the company's success. Utilize various recruitment channels, from traditional job postings to *social media platforms, focusing on those that align best with the type of candidates you are looking for. For example, leveraging LinkedIn can be particularly effective for reaching professionals who may not be actively looking for a job but are open to exciting opportunities. Investing in recruitment technologies like applicant tracking systems can also streamline the hiring process, making it more efficient and effective at attracting top candidates, which is crucial for driving business growth.

Retention strategies are vital for keeping valuable team members engaged and motivated. High employee turnover can be costly and disruptive, mainly when you are in a significant growth phase. To keep your team stable and motivated, create a positive work environment where employees feel valued and part of the company's success. This can be achieved through competitive compensation packages and non-financial means such as career development opportunities, recognition programs, and a supportive workplace culture. Regular feedback and open communication channels can also enhance employee satisfaction by making team members feel heard and involved in decision-making. Providing opportunities for professional growth through training programs or access to courses can also help employees advance their skills and career prospects, which benefits your business by enhancing their productivity and innovation.

Leadership development within your team is crucial in driving and managing growth. As your business expands, the need for strong leadership skills at all levels of your organization becomes more critical. Developing leadership capabilities within your team involves identifying potential leaders early and providing them with the training and experiences they need to succeed in leadership roles. This might include leadership development programs, mentoring, and rotational assignments that allow emerging leaders to gain experience in various aspects of the business. Encouraging a leadership culture where risk-taking is rewarded, and leaders are expected to mentor others can foster leadership skills across your organization. Effective leadership drives business growth by ensuring that teams are motivated, resources are managed efficiently, and business goals are met. It creates a strong foundation for scaling operations and navigating expansion challenges with confidence and vision.

Focusing on these strategic aspects of team building and management as you prepare for and execute business growth ensures that your most valuable asset—your people—are fully aligned and capable of supporting your business's ambitions. This alignment is essential for achieving short-term goals and laying the groundwork for sustained success and scalability. As you move forward, remember that your team's structure, recruitment, retention, and leadership development are not static processes but areas of ongoing focus and adjustment, reflecting the dynamic nature of your growing business.

9.5 STRATEGIC PARTNERSHIPS AND ALLIANCES FOR EXPANSION

Expanding your business often means looking beyond the confines of your current operations and considering how strategic partnerships and alliances can propel your growth objectives forward. Identifying the right partners involves more than just aligning with other businesses that share your market space; it requires a deep understanding of how potential partners' capabilities, resources, and strategic goals complement your own. You can begin by outlining clear criteria that potential partners should meet, including technological capabilities, market presence, or customer base. It's also crucial to evaluate potential partners' financial health and reputation in the industry, as these factors can significantly impact the partnership's success. Tools like business intelligence platforms can provide insights into these aspects, helping you make informed decisions. Additionally, engaging with your network for recommendations or using industry-specific databases can help you effectively identify and vet potential partners.

Forming strategic alliances requires careful negotiation and a clear mutual understanding of the goals and expectations of the partnership. Best practices for creating these alliances include developing a shared vision and objectives that benefit all parties involved. It is essential to approach negotiations with transparency and a spirit of collaboration rather than competition. Drafting a detailed agreement that outlines each party's contributions, responsibilities, and profit-sharing arrangements is crucial. This agreement should also include conflict resolution strategies and exit provisions, ensuring the partnership can adapt or dissolve without significant disruption to your business. Engaging legal counsel during these negotiations can ensure that all agreements are sound and your business's interests are protected.

Once an alliance is formed, managing and nurturing the partnership is critical to long-term success. Regular communication and joint meetings can help maintain alignment and promptly address issues. Setting up project management teams that include members from both parties can enhance collaboration and streamline the execution of joint initiatives. It's also beneficial to establish performance metrics from the outset to monitor the effectiveness of the partnership and make adjustments as necessary. These metrics should focus on financial outcomes and other indicators, such as customer satisfaction and market reach, providing a holistic view of how the alliance contributes to mutual growth objectives.

Leveraging partnerships effectively involves integrating partners into your current business operations and exploring new avenues for mutual growth and expansion. This could mean co-developing new products, entering new markets, or sharing resources to improve operational efficiency. For example, a partnership between a technology firm and a manufacturing company might lead to the development of innovative, tech-driven products that could only be achieved with collaboration. Marketing collaborations can also broaden your reach, allowing both businesses to tap into each other's customer bases and market expertise.

By actively seeking opportunities to innovate and expand through your partnerships, you can achieve growth that is both sustainable and synergistic, driving value for your business and your partners.

Strategic partnerships and alliances are powerful tools for business expansion, offering opportunities to leverage combined strengths for mutual benefit. By carefully selecting partners, forming well-crafted alliances, managing relationships effectively, and continuously seeking opportunities to leverage these partnerships for growth, you can significantly enhance your business's scope and impact in the market.

Moving forward, the next chapter will delve into the innovative strategies for marketing and customer engagement in the digital age, exploring how modern technologies and platforms can be harnessed to drive growth and build deeper connections with your audience. This exploration will give you the tools to reach a wider audience and engage them effectively, turning interest into loyalty and transactions into lasting relationships.

CHAPTER 10

CULTIVATING LONG-TERM SUCCESS

Imagine your business as a vibrant ecosystem, where innovation and creativity are the sunlight and water that nourish it, allowing it to flourish and adapt to the ever-changing environment. Just as gardeners must evolve their techniques to cater to the shifting seasons, a business leader must foster an environment where innovation thrives, ensuring the business survives and thrives in the competitive market landscape. This chapter delves into the critical elements of nurturing an innovative mindset within your company, implementing strategies that foster continuous innovation, staying ahead of industry trends, and effectively measuring the impact of these innovations on your business's growth and sustainability.

10.1 INNOVATING WITHIN YOUR BUSINESS

Fostering an Innovation Mindset: Creating a culture that encourages innovation and creativity.

Cultivating an innovation mindset starts with leadership. As a leader, your openness to new ideas and willingness to take calculated risks sets the tone for your team. It involves creating a company culture that doesn't just allow but encourages creative thinking and experimentation. This can be implemented through regular brainstorming sessions where all employees are encouraged to voice new ideas without fear of judgment or failure. Consider Google's famous '20% time' policy, which allows engineers to work one day a week on projects that are not necessarily in their job descriptions. Such policies can lead to significant innovations, such as Gmail and AdSense. By valuing creativity and flexibility, you encourage your team to bring forward ideas that could transform aspects of your business.

Innovation Strategies: Practical strategies for continuous innovation within your operations and offerings

To embed innovation into your business operations, integrate it into your business strategy and daily practices. This can be achieved through continuous improvement programs that encourage new ways to enhance products and streamline processes. Implementing an agile methodology can also foster innovation. This iterative approach to project management and software development encourages teams to reflect on ways to continuously improve product development and customer satisfaction. Another practical strategy is setting aside a budget for innovation activities. This financial commitment can help experiment with new ideas through prototypes or pilot programs, significantly reducing the risks of scaling untested ideas.

Staying Ahead of Trends: Keeping abreast of industry trends to inform innovation

In a rapidly changing world, staying informed about industry trends is crucial for maintaining a competitive edge. You can use industry reports, attend leading conferences, and participate in relevant webinars to keep up-to-date with the latest developments in your field. Tools like Google Alerts can also provide real-time updates on specific topics related to your business. Moreover, engaging with your customers through social media listening tools can provide insights into consumer behavior and emerging trends. This proactive approach to gathering information will inspire innovative ideas and help you anticipate market shifts, allowing you to adapt your business strategies effectively.

Measuring Innovation Impact: Tools and metrics to measure the impact of innovation on your business

To understand the effectiveness of your innovation efforts, it's essential to be able to measure their impact. This can be done through various metrics such as the number of new products developed, the percentage of revenue from new products, or the efficiency improvements in processes. Tools like innovation audit surveys and balanced scorecards can help quantify innovation's contribution to meeting strategic objectives. Additionally, customer feedback[1]can provide direct insights into how innovations are perceived. Collecting and analyzing this data enables you to validate current innovations' success and guides future innovation initiatives.

Reflective Exercise: Evaluating Your Innovation Strategy

To actively engage with your innovation strategy, consider this reflective exercise:

- **Reflect on your last significant business innovation**: What was it? How did it originate? What impact has it had on your business?

- **Evaluate your innovation culture**: Do your employees feel comfortable presenting new ideas? How is creativity rewarded within your organization?

- **Assess the effectiveness of your innovation processes**: Are there transparent processes for evaluating and implementing new ideas? How quickly can your organization react to new opportunities?

- **Plan for future innovations**: What are the next significant trends in your industry? How can you align your innovation strategy to take advantage of these trends?

Engaging with these questions periodically can help maintain a dynamic approach to innovation, ensuring your business remains relevant and competitive in an ever-evolving marketplace. As you move forward, remember that innovation is not just about significant breakthroughs but also minor, continuous improvements that keep your business agile and responsive to new challenges and opportunities.

10.2 BUILDING A CULTURE OF CONTINUOUS IMPROVEMENT

Principles of Continuous Improvement: Introduction to the principles and benefits of continuous improvement.

In the dynamic business landscape, continuous improvement is a pivotal strategy for maintaining competitiveness and enhancing operational efficiency. They are rooted in the Kaizen philosophy, which originated in Japan, the principle of constant improvement centers around the idea that small, ongoing positive changes can reap significant improvements. Essentially, it's about not being complacent. Whether streamlining an operational process or enhancing customer service protocols, the goal is to make incremental improvements regularly. This approach helps refine processes and fosters a workplace culture that values proactive problem-solving and efficiency. The benefits range from cost reduction and productivity enhancement to employee satisfaction and customer loyalty. When employees see that their minor improvements are valued, it boosts their morale and commitment to the organization's goals. Moreover, in customer-facing operations, the agility to improve and adapt continuously can lead to higher customer satisfaction, as services and products can rapidly evolve to meet changing customer needs.

Implementing Continuous Improvement: Steps to implement a continuous improvement process in your business.

Implementing a continuous improvement process starts with setting a clear, achievable goal. This could be reducing waste, improving customer response times, or enhancing product quality.

Once the goal is set, the next step is communicating this objective to all team members. Everyone must understand not only what the goals are but also why they are essential. This clarity helps align the team's efforts and foster a shared commitment to the process. The next phase involves mapping out existing workflows to identify bottlenecks or waste. This can be achieved through tools like flowcharts or value stream mapping. Engaging team members directly involved in these processes often provides valuable insights into where improvements can be made. After identifying potential areas for enhancement, brainstorm solutions with your team. Encourage creative thinking and consider all suggestions, no matter how small. They are testing these solutions on a small scale before full implementation, which helps assess their effectiveness and make necessary adjustments. Finally, standardize the successful strategies as part of your everyday operations and continuously monitor their effectiveness. This cycle of planning, doing, checking, and acting forms the backbone of a robust, continuous improvement process.

Employee Engagement: Engaging employees in the process of continuous improvement.

Employee engagement in continuous improvement is critical, as the insights and cooperation of those who work with processes daily are invaluable. To effectively engage employees, create an environment where their ideas are welcomed and valued. This can be facilitated through regular team meetings dedicated to discussing efficiency and improvement ideas. Recognizing and rewarding employees who contribute effectively to improvements can also significantly boost engagement. This could be through acknowledgments in team meetings, performance bonuses, or even career advancement opportunities. Additionally, providing training that equips employees with the skills to identify inefficiencies and implement solutions can empower them to contribute more effectively. For instance, training in lean management techniques or problem-solving strategies can give employees the tools to participate in continuous improvement actively. It's also beneficial to involve employees in the results of their suggestions, showing them how their input has led to positive changes. This validates their effort and encourages a continuous cycle of improvement.

Tracking Progress and Results: Methods for tracking improvements and assessing impact on business performance.

To ensure that the continuous improvement processes effectively contribute to business goals, tracking progress and assessing the impact is essential. Setting key performance indicators (KPIs) for specific improvement goals is a start. For example, if the goal is to reduce operational costs, KPIs might include measures like the percentage reduction in waste materials or a decrease in overtime costs. Utilizing business intelligence tools can help track these KPIs by providing real-time data analysis. Regularly reviewing these metrics allows you to measure the success of implemented improvements and identify areas that may need further adjustment. Additionally, periodic audits of the improvement processes can help evaluate their overall effectiveness and alignment with business objectives. Feedback from employees and customers can also provide insightful data on areas for further improvement, ensuring that the continuous improvement process continually evolves and adapts to new challenges and opportunities.

10.3 LEVERAGING BUSINESS ANALYTICS FOR STRATEGIC DECISIONS

Understanding the role of business analytics in strategic decision-making is akin to navigating a ship with a sophisticated navigation system. Just as a captain uses radars and GPS to make informed decisions about the course to steer, you can use business analytics to guide your company through the competitive seas of the market. Business analytics provides you with data-driven insights that help make informed decisions that can significantly impact your business, from marketing strategies to operational efficiencies and customer service improvements. Essentially, business analytics turns data—your business's track record—into insight and insight into foresight, allowing you to anticipate market trends, customer needs, and potential challenges before they fully emerge.

Business analytics tools and techniques have evolved tremendously, offering capabilities that can slice and dice data in valuable ways. For example, predictive analytics can forecast future trends based on historical data, helping you anticipate changes in customer behavior or market conditions. Tools like Tableau or Microsoft Power BI enable you to visualize complex datasets in digestible, graphical formats, making it easier to spot patterns, trends, and outliers. For deeper insights, techniques like data mining and machine learning can analyze large data sets to identify more subtle correlations and causations that might not appear at first glance. Suppose you're running an online retail business; by analyzing customer purchase data and browsing behavior, you can identify which products are frequently bought together and develop bundled offers, enhancing your cross-selling strategies.

Developing a data-driven strategy involves more than just gathering information; it's about integrating this knowledge into your business operations and strategic planning. You can start by identifying key performance indicators (KPIs) that align with your business objectives. These KPIs could range from financial metrics like revenue and profit margins to customer-centric metrics like customer lifetime value and churn rate. Once these KPIs are defined, use your analytics tools to track them consistently and set up dashboards that provide a real-time view of these metrics. This setup enables you to make swift decisions based on the latest data. For instance, if you notice a sudden drop in customer retention rates, you can quickly delve deeper to understand the causes—

perhaps an issue with product quality or customer service—and address these immediately before they impact your business more broadly.

Establishing continuous learning and adaptation processes based on data analytics is crucial for maintaining a competitive edge. This means looking at what the numbers say and understanding why they say it and how you can improve them. It involves creating a cycle of feedback and improvement where data from business operations is continuously collected, analyzed, and fed back into the system to refine processes, products, and strategies. For example, if analytics reveal that customers from a particular geographic region have a high churn rate, further investigation might reveal specific service or product preferences. Using this information, you can tailor your offerings to better meet this segment's needs, thereby reducing churn and increasing customer satisfaction.

Moreover, fostering a data-centric culture within your organization is pivotal. Please encourage teams across your business to use data in their day-to-day decisions. This might mean training employees to use analytics tools effectively or incorporating data-driven insights into regular team meetings and strategic discussions. By democratizing data access and encouraging its use throughout the organization, you ensure that data-driven decision-making becomes a core component of your company's culture, driving innovation and efficiency at every level. As your business continues to grow and evolve, the insights gleaned from business analytics will become an indispensable part of your strategic toolkit, helping you to navigate the complexities of the market with confidence and precision.

10.4 PERSONAL DEVELOPMENT FOR ENTREPRENEURS: GROWING WITH YOUR BUSINESS

Self-Assessment: Regular self-assessment to identify areas for personal development

As you steer the ship of your burgeoning enterprise, it's easy to get lost in the day-to-day demands and overlook your growth as a leader and innovator. However, self-assessment is a crucial tool that ensures you keep pace with your business's growth and lead by example. Regularly taking stock of your skills, strengths, and areas where you can improve is vital. This could be as simple as setting aside time each week to reflect on your recent decisions, the outcomes they led to, and the lessons you can learn from them. Consider maintaining a leadership journal where you record the events and your responses to them. This practice can help you see patterns in your behavior that might require attention or adjustment. Another effective strategy is seeking feedback from trusted colleagues or mentors who can provide honest insights into your leadership style and effectiveness. They might see blind spots that are not apparent to you. Based on this ongoing feedback, set personal development goals that are specific, measurable, achievable, relevant, and time-bound (SMART). Whether it's improving your communication skills, learning to delegate more effectively, or becoming better at strategic thinking, these goals should align with your aspirations and the needs of your business.

Lifelong Learning: Strategies for continuous learning and keeping skills relevant

In a rapidly evolving business landscape, where new technologies and methodologies can change industry standards overnight, continuous learning is beneficial and essential for staying relevant and competitive.

As an entrepreneur, your commitment to lifelong learning sets the tone for your organization's culture and adaptability to change. Start by identifying critical areas in your industry and business management that are rapidly evolving and where upskilling is crucial. Then, leverage the plethora of learning resources available today. Online courses from platforms like Coursera or LinkedIn Learning, webinars, workshops, and sector-specific conferences can keep you updated on the latest trends and best practices. Allocate regular time in your schedule for this learning, treating it with the same importance as any business meeting. Another powerful learning strategy is cross-industry learning, which involves exploring how different sectors solve similar problems and applying these insights to your business. This approach broadens your perspective and can spur innovative ideas and solutions that could be game-changers for your business.

Work-Life Balance: Maintaining work-life balance amidst the demands of scaling a business

Achieving work-life balance is particularly challenging when scaling a business, as the lines between personal and professional life can often blur. Yet, maintaining this balance is crucial not only for your well-being but also for sustained business success. It prevents burnout, keeps creativity and motivation high, and supports healthy relationships with family and friends, who are your support network through the ups and downs of entrepreneurship. Clearly define the boundaries between work and personal time to manage this balance. This might mean setting strict work hours and sticking to them, or at least as closely as possible. Use technology to your advantage by setting reminders to take breaks and using apps that limit your access to work emails or messages during family time. Delegation is another key strategy. Trusting your team with more responsibilities takes some burden off your shoulders and empowers them, aiding their development. Finally, I'd like you to make time for activities that rejuvenate you outside of work. Whether it's a hobby, exercise, or spending time with loved ones, these activities can provide a much-needed counterbalance to the demands of your business.

Networking and Mentorship: Leveraging networking and mentorship for personal growth and development

Networking and mentorship are invaluable to personal and business growth, providing fresh insights, advice, and opportunities to propel your personal development and your business's success. Engage actively in industry associations, business forums, and online communities to connect with peers with similar challenges and ambitions. These platforms offer potential business opportunities and a wealth of collective knowledge and experience that you can tap into. About mentorship, please look for relationships with individuals whose achievements and qualities you have. A good mentor can offer guidance, support, and an objective perspective that is crucial when making difficult decisions or navigating challenging times. Remember, mentorship is a two-way street; it's about building a relationship that benefits both mentor and mentee. I'd like you to be proactive in these relationships, be prepared with questions, and be open to feedback. In return, share your experiences and insights. Networking and mentorship should be viewed not just as avenues for business growth but as vital components of your personal development strategy as an entrepreneur, helping you to refine your leadership style, expand your understanding of your industry, and enhance your ability to guide your business to new heights.

10.5 CREATING A LEGACY: PLANNING FOR THE FUTURE OF YOUR BUSINESS

Building a legacy with your business goes beyond achieving financial success; it's about creating lasting impacts that resonate well after you've stepped down. Starting with a clear vision for the future is crucial. This vision should encapsulate what you want your business to achieve in the market and the values and principles you hope it will stand for. Think of this vision as a guiding star, not just for strategic decisions but also for inspiring your team and aligning stakeholders. Crafting this vision involves deep reflection on the broader impact you want your business to have on society and your industry. For instance, if you are in the technology sector, your vision might include striving to be at the forefront of sustainable practices, influencing your operations, and setting industry standards.

Succession planning is another critical aspect of ensuring the longevity of your business. This process involves identifying and preparing future leaders to take over your business, ensuring its continuity, and preserving its ethos. You can begin by identifying potential leaders within your organization who embody the company's values and have shown both the aptitude and the commitment to lead. Developing these individuals often requires a tailored approach involving mentorship programs, leadership training, and gradually increasing their responsibilities to prepare them for future roles. Additionally, consider the legal and financial aspects of succession planning, including estate planning, ownership transfer, and leadership transition, which are crucial for a smooth changeover. Engaging with legal and financial advisors to map out these aspects can safeguard the business against future disputes or challenges.

Integrating social responsibility into your business practices is not just about enhancing your company's image; it's a commitment to a positive impact that can significantly influence your legacy. This integration can be manifested in various ways, depending on your industry and capabilities. It might involve adopting eco-friendly practices, engaging in community development, or ensuring fair labor practices across your supply chain. These initiatives should align with your business's core operations and objectives, making social responsibility a seamless aspect of your business model rather than a peripheral activity. For instance, if your business is in manufacturing, reducing waste or recycling materials can positively contribute to the environment while potentially lowering costs.

Building a lasting brand means creating one that transcends your leadership and becomes a standalone symbol of trust and quality in the market. This involves consistently delivering on your brand promises and maintaining a strong customer connection through excellent service and continuous engagement. It also means staying relevant by adapting to changing market conditions and evolving consumer expectations while maintaining your core values. Cultivating a strong brand involves meticulous attention to how your business communicates, operates, and engages with its stakeholders, ensuring consistency and alignment with your long-term vision. For example, consistently reinforcing your commitment to quality and customer satisfaction through every product, campaign, and interaction can solidify your brand's reputation, making it a trusted name that customers turn to, generation after generation.

As we conclude this exploration into creating a lasting legacy for your business, remember that the efforts you put in today to define your vision, plan for succession, integrate social responsibility, and build a resilient brand are the seeds you plant for a future that could outlast your tenure. These elements are not just strategies for longevity but are testaments to a business philosophy that values sustainability, ethical responsibility, and visionary leadership. As we transition into the next chapter, we will delve deeper into the strategies for maintaining and growing customer relationships, which are vital for sustaining the legacy and ensuring the continuity of the business in a competitive and ever-evolving market.

CONCLUSION

As we draw the curtains on this journey of empowerment and possibility, let's revisit the core message that has been the backbone of our discussions: **Anyone can start and succeed in their own business with the right habits and mindset.** This book wasn't just about sharing knowledge; it was about transforming the way you see opportunities and challenges in the realm of entrepreneurship.

We've traversed together through the essential stages of starting a business—from cultivating an entrepreneurial mindset that shifts you from dreamer to doer to validating your business idea against the rough tides of the market. We've navigated the complexities of business planning, discussed strategic financing, and highlighted the art of branding and marketing that resonates with your audience. Together, we've explored effective strategies for managing growth and scaling your business to new heights.

Remember, the path of entrepreneurship is strewn with challenges, but each obstacle is a stepping stone to more excellent knowledge and resilience. Embrace these challenges as opportunities to learn and grow. The tools, templates, and frameworks provided in this book are your compass—they are designed to be applied directly to your ventures, helping you to navigate through turbulent waters with confidence and skill.

Now, I urge you **to take that** first **step**. Whether conducting thorough market research, sketching out a business plan, or simply brainstorming potential business ideas, the action you take today is the foundation of your future success. Approach these actions with optimism and a clear vision of the business you will build—one that not only seeks financial success but also enriches your life and contributes positively to the world around you.

Reflecting on my journey of buying a failing company and turning it into a trailblazer in hospital-grade air purification, then moving on to establish multiple successful ventures, I am reminded daily of the lessons learned, the resilience required, and the profound satisfaction that comes from overcoming the odds. Each challenge faced was a lesson that helped sculpt a successful path forward.

As you stand on the threshold of your entrepreneurial journey, remember that the road ahead is illuminated by your ambition, guided by the strategies we've shared, and supported by the community we've built. **You have the power to mold your future, to turn challenges into victories, and to achieve the entrepreneurial success you dream of.**

Let this be your rallying cry: Go forward with courage, heart, and an unwavering determination to succeed. The world of entrepreneurship is ripe with opportunities for those who dare to seize them. **You are ready**—more than ready—to take this on. Let's make those dreams a reality.

REFERENCES

8 Time Management Strategies for Entrepreneurs to Boost… https://yourstory.
com/2023/04/entrepreneur-time-management-tips

A Guide to Building a More Resilient Business https://hbr.
org/2020/07/a-guide-to-building-a-more-resilient-business

The Ultimate Guide to S.M.A.R.T. Goals https://www.forbes.com/advisor/
business/smart-goals/

Strategy Under Uncertainty https://hbr.org/1997/11/strategy-under-uncertainty

How to Build a Compelling Value Proposition (4 Simple Steps) https://
underscore.vc/how-to-write-a-value-proposition/#:~:

Why the Lean Start-Up Changes Everything https://hbr.org/2013/05/
why-the-lean-start-up-changes-everything

5 Low-Budget Market Research Options https://www.driveresearch.com/
market-research-company-blog/5-low-budget-market-research-options/

15+ examples of successful MVPs https://www.rst.software/
blog/15-examples-of-successful-mvps

Write your business plan https://www.sba.gov/business-guide/
plan-your-business/write-your-business-plan.

7 Financial Forecasting Methods to Predict… - HBS Online https://online.hbs.
edu/blog/post/financial-forecasting-methods

Use these 9 KPIs to grow your business faster - QuickBooks https://quickbooks.intuit.com/r/financial-management/the-7-most-important-kpis-to-track-as-a-small-business/

5 Best Risk Management Strategies https://www.sba.gov/blog/5-best-risk-management-strategies

The Definitive Guide on How to Bootstrap Your Startup https://neilpatel.com/blog/bootstrap-startup/

Early-Stage Investing: Angel Investor vs. Venture Capitalist https://www.britannica.com/money/venture-capitalist-angel-investing#:~

6 examples of crowdfunding successes and why they worked https://uk.indeed.com/career-advice/career-development/examples-of-crowdfunding

Grants | U.S. Small Business Administration https://www.sba.gov/funding-programs/grants

5 Branding Tools for Startups https://zebranding.com/blog/5-branding-tools-for-startups/

The Power Of Storytelling For Your Business https://www.forbes.com/sites/theyec/2023/06/08/the-power-of-storytelling-for-your-business-unleashing-your-inner-storyteller/

*Color Psychology in Branding: The Persuasive...*https://www.ignytebrands. com/the-psychology-of-color-in-branding/

*How to Create a Great Social Media Strategy in 2024 (+New...*https://blog.hubspot.com/marketing/social-media-strategy-for-your-business

How to Create an Effective SEO Strategy in 2023 https://www.entrepreneur.com/growing-a-business/how-to-create-an-effective-seo-strategy-in-2023/455357

8 Social Media Success Stories to Inspire You https://www.singlegrain.com/social-media/8-social-media-success-stories-to-inspire-you/

7 Data-Backed Strategies for Boosting Email Conversion Rates https://inbound.human.marketing/how-to-increase-email-conversion-rates

Guerrilla Marketing: An In-Depth Guide for Small Businesses https://
www.fool.com/the-ascent/small-business/marketing-automation/
guerrilla-marketing/

Office ergonomics: Your how-to guide https://www.mayoclinic.org/
healthy-lifestyle/adult-health/in-depth/office-ergonomics/art-20046169

8 Top Business Automation Tools to Use in 2023 https://automateddreams.com/
blog/8-top-business-automation-tools-to-use-in-2023/

*How Standard Operating Procedures (SOPs) Help Startups Get Traction and
Scale Fast* https://www.waybook.com/blog/how-standard-operating-
procedures-sops-help-startups-get-traction-and-scale-fast

6 Ways Outsourcing Can Benefit Your Early Startup https://www.startupgrind.
com/blog/6-ways-outsourcing-can-benefit-your-early-startup/

Best Accounting Software for Small Businesses of April 2024 https://www.
nerdwallet.com/best/small-business/accounting-software

*THE 6 BEST CASH FLOW MANAGEMENT
SOFTWARE*...https://takethehelm.app/blog/
the-6-best-cash-flow-management-software-tools-for-small-businesses/

9 Foolproof Strategies for Profit Margin Improvement https://www.kimonix.com/
post/profit-margin-improvement

5 Tax Planning Strategies for Small Businesses https://www.lendingtree.com/
business/year-end-tax-planning-strategies/

Scaling Your Business: 11 Key Metrics Every Leader Should Monitor
https://www.forbes.com/sites/forbesbusinesscouncil/2023/04/19/
scaling-your-business-11-key-metrics-every-leader-should-monitor/

Market research and competitive analysis https://www.sba.gov/business-guide/
plan-your-business/market-research-competitive-analysis

*Diversification As A Key Strategy For Resilience And Growth In
Business* https://www.forbes.com/sites/jiawertz/2024/03/15/
diversification-as-a-key-strategy-for-resilience-and-growth-in-business/

Grow Your Business with a Strategic Partnership - SCORE.org https://www.
score.org/resource/blog-post/grow-your-business-a-strategic-partnership

Examples of Companies with Successful Innovation Strategies https://www. spyre.
group/post/examples-of-companies-with-successful-innovation-strategies

How continuous improvement can build a competitive edge https://
www.mckinsey.com/capabilities/people-and-organizational-
performance/our-insights/the-organization-blog/
how-continuous-improvement-can-build-a-competitive-edge

The Importance of Business Analytics in Decision-Making https://iabac.org/blog/
the-importance-of-business-analytics-in-decision-making#

ABOUT THE AUTHOR

Marquis Whos' Who Honors Jon Spranger for Launching Three Companies from Scratch and Building Them into Highly Successful and Highly Profitable Companies through Total Company Management and Marketing.

Jon has dedicated over five decades to his profession, showcasing a remarkable journey that spans various industries, primarily focusing on total company management and marketing. Jon's role encompasses a wide range of responsibilities, from ensuring the success of his companies to overseeing operations and providing management consulting services. His experience and dedication have been instrumental in steering his companies toward achieving their goals and maintaining their reputation for excellence.

In addition to his long-standing tender as President of Mason Engineering and Designing Corporation, Jon founded and held the position of President of Alpha Electronics International Inc. from 1988 to 2010.

During this period, he led the company in significant technological advancements and expansions, contributing to its status as a leader in the electronics industry. Furthermore, between 1974 and 2010, Jon founded and held the position of President of Omega Properties, Ltd., where he applied his sharp business acumen to the commercial real estate market and achieved substantial profitability and growth.

All three of Jon's entrepreneurial ventures have resulted in remarkable success, exceeding profitability under his leadership. A testament to his business savvy was the 1.2 million plus dollars that he made when he sold his first property, marking a significant milestone in his career and highlighting his ability to identify and capitalize on investment opportunities. Jon's forward-thinking perspective and emphasis on positive outcomes have been critical factors in navigating through any adversity and continuing to thrive in his endeavors.

Outside of his professional life, Jon is actively involved with Willow Creek Church, reflecting his commitment to civic engagement and community service.

www.ingramcontent.com/pod-product-compliance
Lightning Source LLC
Chambersburg PA
CBHW031856200326
41597CB00012B/436